HIS NAME IS

Cwiz

HIS NAME IS

Cwiz

Lessons from a Lifelong Friendship

JEREMY RHYNE

CIRCUIT BREAKER BOOKS

Circuit Breaker Books LLC
Portland, OR
www.circuitbreakerbooks.com

This is a work of creative nonfiction. The events are portrayed to the best of the author's memory. While all the stories in this book are true, some names and identifying details have been changed to protect the privacy of the people involved.

Rubber chicken image by bodnarphoto/stock.adobe.com
Book design by Vinnie Kinsella

ISBN: 978-1-953639-02-8
eISBN: 978-1-953639-03-5
LCCN: 2020922401

For Cwiz and Jenna
and
for Eli, Miller, and Piper
(when the time is right)

CONTENTS

Foreword   xi
Prologue   1

The School Years

Chapter 1. Who Does That?   7
Chapter 2. Can Do   11
Chapter 3. Bando   17
Chapter 4. The Good Neighbor Discount   21
Chapter 5. Send in the Clown   25
Chapter 6. Teacher's Aide   31
Chapter 7. Airport Shenanigans   35
Chapter 8. The Tycoon   39
Chapter 9. Permanent Record   43

Adulthood?

Chapter 10. Flatbed Pool Party   49
Chapter 11. Concrete Missionary   55
Chapter 12. The Valet Days   59
Chapter 13. Paint Gun Attack   63
Chapter 14. The Kidnapping   71
Chapter 15. The Scott Head   75
Chapter 16. Never More Happy   79
Chapter 17. The Funniest Dude in the Room   83
Chapter 18. Stop Hugging the Guests   87
Chapter 19. Skinny-Dipping in the Dancing Waters   89
Chapter 20. How Lovely Are Thy Branches   93
Chapter 21. The Juice   97
Chapter 22. You Guys a Couple of Clowns?   105
Chapter 23. Jerry-Rigging   109

Chapter 24. For the Free Cream 113
Chapter 25. Selling Jeeps 117
Chapter 26. Negative Machismo 121
Chapter 27. Baptizing Flipper 125
Chapter 28. I Pity the Fool 129
Chapter 29. The Terrorist 133
Chapter 30. Lookuphere! 137
Chapter 31. Traffic School 139
Chapter 32. Has This Been Laundered? 143

The Roaming Years

Chapter 33. In All His Glory 147
Chapter 34. The Vomitfoil 151
Chapter 35. Have You Ever Been in a Turkish Prison? 155
Chapter 36. Egyptian Brawl 161
Chapter 37. Baboon Brawl 169
Chapter 38. Southeast Asia 175
Chapter 39. The Stank in Here Is Unreal 183
Chapter 40. Grace's Son 189

Thirtysomething

Chapter 41. Calico Jones 195
Chapter 42. Prom Trip 199
Chapter 43. Nana Sandwiches 203
Chapter 44. Central Park Date with Steve-O 207
Chapter 45. Game Show Lovin' 209
Chapter 46. Here Comes the Fudge 213
Chapter 47. Montana 217
Chapter 48. Snakebit 225

Getting It Together

Chapter 49. The Complete Package 233
Chapter 50. Via Chicago 239
Chapter 51. The Reverse Surprise Birthday Party 241
Chapter 52. Maui'd 245

Chapter 53. Magnetic Personality   249
Chapter 54. Remodel Surprise   253
Chapter 55. The Skinny on Tio Flaco's Tacos   255
Chapter 56. The Chicken Man Cometh   257
Chapter 57. America's Pastime–Heckling   261
Chapter 58. Swimming with Sea Pigs   263
Chapter 59. The Honeymooners   267
Chapter 60. Snake Eyes   273
Chapter 61. A Memorable Meal   277
Chapter 62. Making Memories   281

Epilogue   287
Acknowledgments   289
Appendix. The Adventures of Calico Jones   293

You've heard it said, perhaps in a television commercial, "*What do you get the man who has everything?*" This question, which sprang into my mind every time my friend's birthday came around, motivated me to write this book.

For several years, Caesar Ruiz (whom we all call Cwiz—pronounced *Quiz*), had been telling me he wanted to find a way to record "the stories," or "our stories," to preserve them for all time. He would lament his failing memory ("*My memory is so horrible*"), worried that the good times we had were fading away like a neglected campfire. Once the details of the stories were lost, what would we have to pass on to our children?

Cwiz even suggested at one point that we get all the guys together for a weekend, hire a video crew, and tell the stories to rolling cameras so we could have the memories laid down once and for all. When he talked about this, it appeared he was fueled by his desire to ensure that his three kids (Eli, Miller, and Piper) heard these stories about him, so they would be able to absorb all of the crazy fun he (and we) had.

When his birthday rolled around again a couple summers ago, after considering various $50 gifts I could pick up at the mall, I suddenly realized that there actually *was* one thing I could get the guy who had everything.

I could write down his stories and present him with a book of his own folklore.

They say a good friend knows your stories, but a best friend lives them with you. I certainly knew Cwiz's stories, but I had lived most of them, too. I have been friends with Cwiz for over thirty years. We met in high school, spent most of our high school and college years goofing off, traveled overseas together, were in each other's weddings, and, most recently, we have watched each other create families. I was in as good a position as anyone to write the stories. And where my memory was sparse, or where I had not been present, I could meet with the people who were there and mine their memories for more detail.

My goal in writing this book was primarily to preserve the hilarious stories of our youth. But I was also interested in ferreting out some of Cwiz's originality, hoping to uncover some truths about living life that will speak to all of us.

As you will see, particularly in his early years, Cwiz was by no means perfect. He certainly rubbed some people the wrong way as he awkwardly explored how to use his unique energies. He was often reckless and sometimes hurt himself. At other times he was just plain dumb, and occasionally, he had minor brushes with the law.

Despite the rougher edges of his budding personality, Cwiz's faults were also his unmatched strengths. Here was a guy who appeared to be utterly immune to the fear of failure, who was willing to push his chips out and lay it all out on the line, certain he would get it back in the end. He always seemed to be playing with house money. And apart from his bold (some would say rash) fearlessness, Cwiz's other strengths made him charming. He has always had a vibrant creativity, a quick wit, and a playful and infectious humor that draws people to him.

At this point in his life, Cwiz has gotten some very important things dialed in. He has figured out how to channel his gifts into a force for good in the world. This book is intended to share some of the lessons he has learned and reveal some of the ways in which he has impacted people's lives for the better, while conveying the ridiculous fun we had along the way. I have tried to fan into flame these old gifts we were given, these old stories of our youth, and present them here for you.

Thanks for the memories, Cwiz.

Every good story seems to begin with a snake.
—NICOLAS CAGE

As his consciousness ascended from a dreamless abyss, Cwiz became aware of a mechanical humming, then an electronic beep. His fledgling awareness immediately turned its focus to the painful throbbing in his left hand. His mind continued to sharpen as it peeled back shadowy layers of morphine and fatigue.

His eyes slowly cracked open and fell on his hospital room. Cwiz now remembered where he was: the intensive care unit of a medical center in Chula Vista, California. He looked at his left hand. It was swollen to twice its normal size and he could barely move his fingers.

Wincing, he turned his left palm down so that he could see the webbing between his thumb and forefinger. He could just make out two tiny pinpricks, the unlikely source of his current predicament. Those two nearly invisible holes in his hand had been the deadly conduits for the injection of a lethal poison. The poison—or, more accurately, venom—had been slowly traveling from his left hand up his left arm for almost twelve hours. The image of two beady rattlesnake eyes came back to him and made him shudder.

His swollen arm bore markings from a black felt pen, marks that perfectly and visibly encapsulated the problem. The first black mark on his wrist noted the time: *11:45 a.m.* A second black mark halfway up to his elbow had a doctor's scrawl next to it: *2 p.m.*, and a third read *4 p.m.* These marks showed the inevitable, deadly progression of the venom as it made its way to his heart. If the venom entered his heart, he would likely die, at the age of thirty-two.

I heard what happened while traveling on a business trip in New Orleans. I received a frantic phone call from our mutual friend Cameron, telling me what Cwiz had done to land himself in the ICU. Floored, I couldn't grasp the idea that Cwiz might be gone when I returned home.

Although he was what you might call a "good church kid" growing up, Cwiz had often been reckless with his personal safety (and sometimes with the safety of others). Despite his careless and sometimes stupid behavior, he had somehow always avoided the worst possibilities, gracefully sidestepping any long-term repercussions. And he had been slow to listen to friends and family who warned him to tone it down or take it easy.

Cwiz's reckless behavior was not traditional. Mind-altering substances never had any pull with him. He never took drugs, and in thirty years of hanging out with him, I have seen him drink alcohol only once or twice.

No, Cwiz's recklessness was far more creative. He wouldn't play with risky pharmaceuticals, but he had no problem playing with deadly serpents to show off. As a result, those who visited Cwiz at the hospital mostly scolded him, telling him repeatedly that he had to get it together, to stop behaving so irresponsibly. "Do you think you're immortal?" they would ask him.

Many of us who had participated with him in his ridiculous antics for years had either literally moved away, or we had moved on with our lives. We had gotten married in our mid-twenties and were now on to our second kids, and in some cases, our second wives. We had jumped off the crazy train, only to occasionally take short weekend rides to Vegas with Cwizzy.

While we were in college getting degrees and in graduate school getting more degrees, Cwiz was wandering the globe, sampling its wonders. He was also honing his skills as a salesman and learning how to make money. By his late twenties, Cwiz began to taste real financial success as a real estate agent, and later, a broker. In his early thirties, he started a construction business. He tried to tone down his antics, as we'd warned him to, but he still tended to take it too far, and this time, he realized it might actually kill him.

As he sat in the ICU, alone, he thought about all of the things he had done in his life. Images passed like a speeding locomotive in his mind's eye. He saw the riot in Vietnam, the sailing in Sydney, and the lonesome wandering in China. He saw himself hanging from a bridge over Iguazu Falls in Brazil, riding horses around the Giza Pyramids, jumping out of a driver's seat into the back of a moving vehicle, crowd surfing, leading chants at a World Cup game in Germany. He saw the fights he had gotten into, the pranks he had played, the brushes with law enforcement, the awards he had won, the untold adventures with the kids he was mentoring at his church, the ridiculously fun times in Vegas with his buddies, and the many, many friendships he had enjoyed. All of these images seemed to now funnel down, pointlessly, to one stupid decision.

He looked again at the highest black mark on his left arm. The venom was now nearly to his shoulder. A tear appeared in his eye. *After everything I've done, I'm going to die from a stupid snakebite.* He almost laughed at how ridiculous it all was, but then the fear resurfaced. In the quiet of his mind, he thought, *If I get out of here, I am going to settle down and stop acting like a clown. I am going to use my gifts to make the world a better place.*

PART ONE

THE SCHOOL YEARS

Me (left) and Cwiz (right), 1989.

CHAPTER 1

WHO DOES THAT?

W e met, at fifteen, in the most insignificant way possible: because our last names both began with "R."

It was the first day of school of my sophomore year at Fountain Valley High School, in Orange County, California. Health class was quiet, and everyone was uncomfortable. My mind was swirling with various questions: *How hard is this class going to be? Is the teacher going to be mean? Do I have any friends in here, or will I make any?*

The students were arranged in their rows of desks in alphabetical order. As fate would have it, as a Rhyne, I was sitting right in front of Caesar Ruiz. Little did I know that I was about to embark on a decades-long adventure with this dude I'd seen around but hadn't met.

While Mrs. Braun was calling roll, starting with the A's, I put my head down on my desk. Then, oddly, I heard some quiet electronic snare drum sounds coming from behind me. I turned around and looked at this guy. He was a little puffy at fifteen years of age, still hanging on to some baby weight. He looked taller than me, with a helmet of brown hair swept up like a surfable wave breaking on one side of his head. He looked at me and unfurled a mischievous smile. I quickly turned back around and waited for Mrs. Braun to call my name.

I heard the electronic drums again as I turned my attention to the teacher, who kept calling roll, each name followed by a sharp "Here."

The drums continued. A snare drum. Then another. Then a bass drum struck. Then a tinny cymbal clanged. Some of the kids around me started looking around, and Mrs. Braun looked up from her roll sheet. The drums stopped. I heard the guy behind me unsuccessfully stifle a snicker.

When Mrs. Braun resumed the roll, I turned around and looked at him again. The guy's eyes widened, and he lifted the cover of his backpack on his desk to show me what was hidden underneath. It was a small synthesizer keyboard with a tiny drum pad on top. Now in on the joke, I tried not to smile.

While Mrs. Braun continued calling roll, I heard him hit the synthesizer keys again, but this time the keys played a pre-recorded message that he had made with his own voice.

The keyboard squawked out the teacher's name, "Mrs. Braun!"

She looked up again, wondering who had said her name. Everyone looked around.

Then he did it again, while she was still trying to figure out who had called her name. Her name rang out when Caesar pressed the keyboard inside of his backpack. And this time, the sound was in a different key, a little higher. He did it over and over again.

"Mrs. Braun!"

"Mrs. Braun!"

"Mrs. Braun!"

"Mrs. Braun!"

"Mrs. Braun!"

Then he started a sort of rap of her name with the keys.

"Muh, muh muh muh muh mmmmmmmmmmmmm, Mrs., Mrs., Mrs., Mrs."

"Mrs. B, Mrs. B, Mrs. B, Mrs. Bruh, Mrs. B, B, B, B."

"Mrs. Braun!"

Her name was called in a rapid computeristic lingo, in a higher key each time, while he ran his finger up the keyboard one key at a time, all while the keyboard remained hidden in his backpack. I dared not look at him.

Mrs. Braun was perplexed, looking around the class wondering what the hell was going on. A general roar erupted in the room, and everyone's eyes fell on Caesar.

I realized immediately that many of my fellow classmates were already in on who this guy was. They had obviously already had some prior experience with Caesar, perhaps during their freshman year. Mrs. Braun walked directly to him, having located the culprit. The backpack was confiscated and deposited in her desk. No doubt the incident was recorded on the school's central file card in the form of at least one hour's detention.

That was my introduction to Cwiz. I marveled at him.

Who does that? On the first day of class?

I decided to see what this guy was all about.

LIFE LESSON:
Make people laugh, and you will make friends.

CHAPTER 2

CAN DO

The front door, which faced southwest toward the beach, was always open (literally open). The breeze blew through the front door, gratifying the house with fresh and salty air. The house Cwiz lived in was a modest four-bedroom tract home, not unlike every other home in Fountain Valley. His house was right next to our church, so we always seemed to be at his place, dropping by, dropping off, picking up, or hanging out.

His mom, Graciela, and his sister, Fabiola, lived with him. Their dog Camila struck me as a terrified little thing that came in and sniffed around the couch from time to time, but mostly stayed clear of me when I was there.

Whenever we came in, Graciela gave us all big smiles and spoke to Cwiz in Argentine Spanish. The love she had for him radiated out of her beaming face. If she could have pinched his cheeks and smushed and kissed his face without embarrassing him in front of us, no doubt she would have.

Cwiz and his mom were close and frequently laughed together about something they were saying, like old friends with inside jokes. I was only two years into my Spanish classes in school, and although I thought I could catch some words here and there, I could never keep up with them. So I smiled and pretended to understand. I remember thinking it was odd that they seemed to relate to each other as equals, as if Cwiz had already earned his mother's trust and respect at the age of sixteen.

Although Cwiz was constantly being hauled into the principal's office in high school, Graciela did not seem fazed by the assessment of other adults that Cwiz was completely "out of control." As he tells it, every teacher he ever had in his life could barely tolerate him. He told me that during grade school, he was incapable of going along with the class and doing what everyone else was doing. For that reason, he was nearly always in trouble.

But one teacher in the fourth grade made an impact. Mrs. Wilkinson figured out how to handle him. She could see he needed some special attention, so she made Cwiz her helper and kept him right next to her as she taught the class. Cwiz became her personal assistant, and he loved her for it.

During a parent/teacher conference that year, Mrs. Wilkinson told Graciela, "Caesar is a wonderfully funny kid. Anyone who is that funny is obviously very bright. He just needs to learn how to tone it down and apply his brainpower, and he will be very successful in life." This insightful comment by Mrs. Wilkinson stuck with Cwiz, and with Graciela. It was something his mother repeated to Cwiz on many occasions when he got into trouble. Whenever he would start to push the boundaries at home, she would remind him, "Remember what Mrs. Wilkinson said? You must learn when to tone it down."

As for his father, Cwiz rarely spoke of him, leaving me to guess for years where his father was and what he was doing. I only knew his parents were divorced, like mine. We did not talk about how or why our parents had split; it was the reality we knew, and we did not dwell on it.

But I met his dad one time in high school, when he suddenly appeared at the house. Cwiz and I were outside on the driveway talking when he pulled up. I could see the surprise on Cwiz's face as his dad's truck slowed down at the curb next to the flat front lawn. The truck he arrived in looked like it was being used as intended. Its mud flaps were caked. The rear fenders behind the back tires had sprayed, dried mud on them. And Cwiz's dad was dressed like he was accustomed to hard, dirty work, with ragged jeans and grease stains on his hands.

He walked slowly over to us, as though he were a little nervous. He said, "Hey there, kid." Cwiz said hey back. Cwiz went inside and told Graciela that his dad was there, and we stayed inside for a bit. His parents talked outside for a little while, Cwiz paying attention to the conversation outside his bedroom window while simultaneously talking to me.

It was Cwiz's birthday that day, but his dad did not say anything about it when he arrived. I asked him if he thought his dad was there for his birthday.

He shook his head. "No."

His dad called out to him, and we went back outside. His dad then wished him happy birthday, but it seemed to me Graciela had just told him about it.

He said, "I got something for you in the truck."

When he walked back from the truck, he was holding a large can of peaches. The colorful can was unwrapped and huge, the size of a volleyball. He handed it to Cwiz, whose hands dropped with the weight of it. Cwiz looked at it thoughtfully.

"Thank you," he said.

Then his dad left.

Many years later, both of us now with our own children, we were traveling together on a boat to Santa Catalina Island to camp with our families. We had an hour or so to talk as the kids ran around, and we took a small booth in the bow with just the two of us. I asked Cwiz if he remembered that day his dad showed up on his birthday. Cwiz said he thought his dad did not know it was his birthday when he showed up, so he just rooted around in his truck for something to give him.

I wondered out loud how a dad could do that.

Cwiz shrugged. He said his dad was a hard man with a long, hard story. He said he grew up very poor in Texas and then joined the Navy as a teenager, joining a unit called the Seabees. The Navy sent him to Vietnam, and life got even harder for him there. He said his dad never really recovered from his experience in the war, and he struggled for years and years to get his mind straight.

They never spoke anymore. Cwiz said he wished they could, because he wanted his dad around to be a grandfather to his kids, even if he could not be a father to him. It occurred to me that Cwiz was long past the point of expecting anything from his dad, and that perhaps even back then on his birthday, he had learned to tolerate this reality without the pain causing him any lasting harm.

When I asked whether he had learned anything from his dad, he said his dad took a sort of tough love approach. He spent weekends with him until he was about fourteen. On those weekends, his dad taught him some pretty intense survival skills. When Cwiz was eleven, his dad took him out to the desert and taught him to drive a manual stick shift while simultaneously firing a handgun out the window of the car at a pretend enemy. His dad was convinced such skills would be critical when the inevitable invasion from a foreign power (probably the Russians) came to our soil. Cwiz would be ready. Cwiz chuckled as he related this story. He said it was weird, but it was clear to him that his dad loved him deep down, in his own strange way.

I said it sounded like those weekends would have been fun for a kid. Cwiz said they were, and the thing that stuck with him was that his dad was constantly talking about having a "Can Do" attitude, which was the motto of the Seabees. His dad showed him how to camp, shoot, hunt, and be the type of person who can tackle any challenge. I noted that Cwiz said all this with pride. He was still proud of his dad in spite of it all.

It was this attitude of confidence that Cwiz chose to cherish from his dad. It would have been easy, and even understandable, for Cwiz to have fallen into some destructive behavior to salve the wound from an emotionally absent dad. No doubt his rambunctious behavior in school had something to do with it. But the behavior never devolved into self-destruction, only attention-seeking. And I am proud of him for that.

From my point of view, the credit goes to his mom, who was more than enough for him, and who propped him up with unbounded affection and support his entire life. She still does.

LIFE LESSON:
You can dwell on the past, or you can choose to let it go.

CHAPTER 3

BANDO

Cwiz was a "bando." That was the term we used at the time to refer to anyone who was a member of the high school band. It was not meant to be a flattering term; it was synonymous with "nerd." Our school had probably one hundred kids in the band, perhaps more, and they had these fantastic blue uniforms with ridiculous military-style epaulettes. The uniform was topped off with a giant dorky hat and a suffocating chin strap. The band put on a half-time show during the Friday night high school football games.

My understanding is that within the band community itself, there were several factions, some cooler than others. The factions occurred naturally, depending on which instrument you played. There was the brass section, the wind section, and percussion. There were also flag girls and drill team members.

Cwiz was in the drum line, but even within that group, there were the cool and the lame. In the drum line, the kids playing the snares were cool, but the bandos playing the giant bass drums or the cymbals were not.

Cwiz played the cymbals. This meant that, whilst dressed up in his uniform, he paraded around the field pursuant to strict choreographical instructions, carrying two giant cymbals, each the size of a truck tire. At rare appointed moments in the song, he would hold up his "instrument" high and bang the cymbals together with a loud, brassy crash. Then he would awkwardly and mechanically parade around the field again until the group lined up into another one of their formations. Then he would bang the cymbals together again. The thought of Cwiz standing there, holding his cymbals high, waiting with eager anticipation for the exact moment in the song to smash them, makes me laugh every time I think about it.

When he was a freshman, his two best friends and neighbors, Chris and Aaron, were band members. They wanted him to join, so they told him there were cute girls on the drill team, and most importantly, the entire band got to go to Disney World for a whole week at the end of the year. That settled it for him. Cwiz decided he would endure the year of band practice and cymbal-crashing if he could go to Florida.

He suffered through the practices all year long and finally got his ticket to Florida. The day before the trip, all the students had to bring their bags to the high school for inspection, and the bags had to be left overnight. The rule was intended to eliminate contraband. After Cwiz left his bags to be checked, a chaperone "band mom" called his house and asked to speak to Graciela.

The band mom said that during their inspection of Cwiz's bag, they found a roll of duct tape, a screwdriver, marakas, several bags of cookies, and some pliers. Graciela asked Cwiz why he was bringing all this strange stuff to Florida.

Cwiz replied, "You never know."

Graciela said, "Maybe it's best to leave them home."

But Cwiz would not be disarmed so easily. Although he arrived at the airport without his tools, he showed up with a sombrero on his head. And not just any sombrero. The sombrero was a full six feet in diameter, and he managed to wear it onto the plane. As he sat in the aisle seat, the sombrero reached the window on his right and all the way to the center seat across the aisle. The plane had not yet taken off, and the band moms were already sick of him.

After some of the people around him complained, they confiscated his sombrero.

Cwiz said, "I thought this was a free country!" and Aaron and Chris cracked up.

The band moms said, "Well, not this week it isn't."

Cwiz yelled out at the band mom as she folded it up and walked back to her seat, "Would you mind checking the sombrero at the gate for me?"

When they finally got their day at Disney World, a band mom was specially assigned to be Cwiz's personal handler to make sure he did not get into any trouble. But when the handler went to the restroom, he ran off and managed to evade her the entire day. The very next day after he got home from Florida, he quit the band. It had served its purpose.

LIFE LESSON:
Set goals and achieve them.

CHAPTER 4

The Good Neighbor Discount

When Cwiz turned sixteen, he showed up to church with his brand-new Chevy Blazer, a gift from his mother. It was shiny and it was fast. I was years away from buying a car of my own, so it was exciting to have a buddy with a brand-new car. Other friends also scored new cars from their parents on their sixteenth birthdays, and we were suddenly thrust into a whole new world of freedom.

We were now free to leave campus at lunch and go out to any restaurant we chose—like adults! It is hard to overestimate the joy this brings to a sixteen-year-old kid, to know they can drive wherever they want. The Blazer became tangible proof of our new-found freedom. There it was, evidence that we could go anywhere and do anything.

That new car smell did not last, however. You might say Cwiz played a little fast and loose with the Blazer, and he was always driving far too fast for his own good. As a result, the Blazer did not last very long. After several car accidents, Graciela took it away, declaring it was "haunted."

One time before the haunting, however, on a rainy day, Cwiz and I took off to Wendy's for a quick lunch. Wendy's was the closest burger joint to the school, so it was our usual spot. Cwiz was keen to see how the slippery streets would impact his beautiful new Blazer's capabilities, and we soon found out. We tore out of the school with the tires struggling to find a hold on the wet pavement. The truck found its grip, and we took off like a rocket. In the passenger's seat, I grabbed the handle above the window and held on tight. We came to a light, stopped fast, and prepared to turn.

After waiting for the traffic to make the right turn, Cwiz punched it, hard, and simultaneously jerked the wheel, with the intent of peeling out around the corner. Instead, the Blazer lost its grip on the pavement, and it spun in a complete 180-degree turn. When we came to a stop, we were facing the other way, perfectly placed in the left-hand turn lane of the opposite lanes. We looked at each other, cracked up, and thought about how lucky we were that no one was parked in that left-hand turn lane. The light turned green almost immediately after we stopped, and we proceeded slowly back the way we came. We ended up going to Wendy's a different way, as if nothing had happened.

We got to the restaurant and flashed our special Good Neighbor discount cards, which my mom had scored because she worked at an advertising agency that did some work for Wendy's. With these special little yellow cards, the cardholder could get 20 percent off the total purchase. Because we went to Wendy's practically every day in high school, the Good Neighbor card probably saved us hundreds of dollars. Over time, the little paper cards became frayed and torn, and eventually they were thrown away.

But whether he had the card or not, every time we pulled up to the drive-through, Cwiz would always finish his order by saying, "And I have a Good Neighbor discount." The discount was always honored. This went on for several years after high school, well into our college years.

Flash forward about thirty years to 2018. Out of the blue, Cwiz sent me a video that he took from his phone while ordering at the exact same Wendy's drive-through that still sits there thirty years later. The video shows a lit-up drive-through menu screen with pictures of hamburgers on it.

Cwiz says: "I'll take a plain cheeseburger, fries, and a Coke, easy ice."

A muffled cracking voice responds: "Okay, we'll have the total for you at the window."

He says, "Oh, and one more thing. I have a Good Neighbor discount."

"Okay, drive to the window, please."

End of video.

I was sitting in court when I got the video, waiting for the judge to take the bench and call my case. I played the video and busted out laughing. A few of my fellow lawyers sitting with me in the gallery shot me a glare. They could not see why someone would utter a guffaw like that in a court of law. I sheepishly put my phone away in my coat pocket and smiled to myself.

LIFE LESSON:
Take a discount as far as it will go.

CHAPTER 5

SEND IN THE CLOWN

During my sophomore year of high school, after my friend Ian (whom we call "the Captain") invited me to the church youth group, I was "saved." Cwiz, having also been recently "saved," was excited about my conversion. We were all fired up about our faith and looking for ways to share it with others. That year, our youth pastor, Gregg, told us about a missions conference for high-schoolers. He said the missions conference was a good way to learn about opportunities to share our faith, and Cwiz and I decided to go.

The weekend-long conference was called Conquest. Only one other student from our church, Reggie, came with us. At the time, Reggie was in the process of writing a book on how to start a Bible study on campus. Reg was a "PK," a pastor's kid, and he was looking to make his mark on the world, like his dad. Reg had massive eyeglasses that made him look smart, which was fitting, because he was (and is) a smart dude.

After we arrived and got settled in the college dorm rooms we'd stay in during the conference, we went to our first session, where we listened to music and a stirring sermon. After the sermon, we went back to our rooms and were bored. Although we were dedicated to a weekend of faith exploration and serious consideration of what God was calling us to do with our lives, we also thought it would be funny if one of us went streaking through the quad. So, as the high school kids milled about the common area of the dorms talking about their decisions to serve on a mission trip that summer, Reg and I went to prep the crowd. We ran into the common area screaming, "Omigahhh, there is some dude streaking in the dorms!"

Everyone turned to see what was going on and, right on cue, Cwiz came running out of the dorm into the common area. He was wearing a bandana on his face like he was an old west outlaw, boxer shorts, and nothing else. For some reason, he screamed, "Cowabungaaaaa!" and ran through the crowd hooting and then ran back into the dorms. Reg and I laughed all the way back to our room, where we found Cwiz rolling on the bed with tears of laughter in his eyes.

We were truly doing the Lord's work.

The second night of the conference, we were impressed with the worship band, which was like any mediocre rock band you might have seen back then, but more Jesus-y and with less hair. The band's wholesome lyrics were published on a screen behind them so you could sing along. After about an hour of moving music, an old man took the podium and began to proclaim the gospel. In particular, he focused on what Christians call the Great Commission. In short, the message that night was: Jesus's last words to us were to go into all the world and make disciples, and what had we done about it? Nothing, that's what.

The speaker's name was Louie Inks. Louie had a white afro styled like a Chia Pet. His gravelly voice carried conviction in the lower register, and he had a natural charisma and power to persuade. Inks ran a missions outfit called Royal Servants International, based in Illinois. Royal Servants' schtick was to take high school students from around the country, train them, and ship them off to Europe on a two-month whirlwind trip to harvest souls for Jesus. The students were trained to gather crowds through puppet shows, clown performances, singing, and drama groups. Once a crowd was gathered, the group of high-schoolers would fan out and try to share the gospel using special religious tracts, written in just about any language you could possibly imagine.

Every summer, Royal Servants was responsible for unleashing hundreds of enthusiastic teenage evangelists on the old continent's World Heritage Sites. Each and every one of these kids was utterly convinced of their unique hold on the truth about God and the afterlife. They were determined to persuade unsuspecting tourists all over Europe that Jesus was the only way they could get into heaven.

Inks was recruiting volunteers for the upcoming summer, and what he said that night sealed it for me. After persuading us that we had done little or nothing to fulfill Jesus's Great Commission, he said:

"If not here, where?"

"If not now, when?"

"If not you, who?"

Those three questions, somehow simple yet still so powerful, breached my outer walls and pierced me to the core.

God is calling me to be a missionary in Europe. The world needs me.

Looking around, and seeing Cwiz and Reggie raising their hands too, I figured this was my calling. That night, I signed up and was proud to announce that I was about to be a Royal Servant. Cwiz, Reg, and I were going to Europe to change the world.

It's totally easy to change the world, you guys, if you know what you're doing. And of course, we knew. I mean, we were in high school, so we had learned a lot about living in the world and stuff. We had literally worked jobs and everything. In fact, I had already worked part time at Arby's when I was fifteen, so I knew a thing or two about human suffering.

After several months of fundraising, our summer of missions work began with a boot camp where we learned how to share the gospel. We woke up at 5:30 every morning, and after a mundane breakfast of Malt-O-Meal, we performed manual labor clearing trails and pulling weeds in the backwoods of Illinois. After the manual labor, we memorized by heart a religious tract called the Four Spiritual Laws.

The trick was that, even though we now had a tract memorized, we needed people to save. So, in the afternoons, we worked on skillsets that would enable us to attract large crowds. And once the crowd was there, we would set the hook with a gospel presentation. So, for a few weeks, we learned how to gather crowds first with clowns and puppets, then with singing, and finally with a drama presentation.

Naturally, Cwiz was a clown for Jesus, which never got old. He put on the makeup and the ridiculous clothes, and being as good as he was, he was designated to perform a solo act. With a song playing from our portable speakers, he came out on stage and danced around like a moron. He had this signature move where he would act like he was entering a home by opening an invisible door and turning on the light. He would mime these huge physical movements, entering the invisible house by stepping over the threshold, each step a full two feet off the ground. When he flipped the invisible light switch, he would look up, but the light evidently did not work. He would keep flipping the switch and looking up, annoyed. For some reason, his act with the light switch was hilarious. Clowning suited him.

When we arrived in Europe with our evangelistic tools perfected, we spent six weeks or so sleeping in campgrounds everywhere and attempting to share the gospel with whoever would listen. We drove in a coach bus through England, France, Belgium, Germany, Switzerland, and Italy, and then back again.

Cwiz's clown act was the opening act and never failed to draw in crowds, particularly families with kids. The little urchins gathered in front of our makeshift stage cackled, thrashed, and rolled around on each other in laughter as Cwiz clowned around. Usually, that was followed up with the puppets. Then Reggie took the stage with about a dozen others and they sang a few songs, usually holding hands. The last act was the drama group (or live action human video put to music), which depicted a pretty grim scenario of a girl suffering from addiction and depression. But never fear! Jesus swept in at the end and saved her. I played the part of Satan in the drama.

So Cwiz clowned, I acted devilish, and Reggie sang in front of Notre Dame, the Eiffel Tower, the Glockenspiel, the Tower of London, and the Vatican (what better place to try to make new

Satan and the clown.

Christians, right?), and in campsites all over Europe. We performed our adolescent hearts out for Jesus all summer long and did the best we could to change Europe's mind about God, one crappy performance at a time.

I am not certain we did much to better people's lives. And I am pretty sure we did little to better the reputation of a dwindling Christian presence in Western Europe. But I am confident about a couple of things. First, the trip solidified a bond between me and Cwiz that would last a lifetime, and for that reason, I am forever grateful we went on that adventure together. Second, the trip opened our eyes to the world at large and instilled in us a lifelong love of travel, which would change our lives in immeasurable ways.

LIFE LESSON:
If you're going to be a clown, be a good one.

CHAPTER 6

Teacher's Aide

Cwiz was not exactly a model student in his high school years. He seemed to be looking ahead, pining for what he would do when he got out of high school. As a result, he looked for ways to enjoy himself while in school. A resourceful fellow, he found like-minded people to assist, even some people who were on the high school staff.

One such person was a teacher named Mr. M. I'll leave out his full name just in case he still teaches there (although he would have to be like 105 by now). There was no shortage of rumors about Mr. M at the school. The main rumor was that he liked to smoke pot with students in his van, which neither Cwiz nor I ever saw firsthand.

But the second and absolutely true rumor circulating around the campus was that you could take Mr. M's class, do nothing at all, and still get a good grade. I can personally attest to the truth of this. Seeking to avoid chemistry, I took Mr. M's oceanography course. The course consisted almost entirely of BBC videos about penguins and polar bears inhabiting the poles of our planet.

Cwiz took his other course, life science, as a senior in high school. It was his second time taking the course. Because he had taken it before, Mr. M figured that even though Cwiz was a student in his course (again), Cwiz could also act as a teacher's aide of sorts. But instead of grading papers and keeping track of assignments like most teacher's aides did, Cwiz was assigned other tasks.

Mr. M had rental property, a condo, not far from the school, and he also happened to have landscaping difficulties on account of some disagreement with his gardener. Mr. M asked Cwiz to handle the problem for him. So, instead of showing up to Mr. M's class, Cwiz would leave school and drive to Mr. M's condo. At the condo, there was a lawnmower in a storage unit. Using Mr. M's key, Cwiz would pull out the mower and mow the lawn around the condo and do some other minor landscaping. When he was done, he would drive back to school and show up to class right before it ended. He would give Mr. M the key, and Mr. M would give him $15. That earned him a passing grade.

One day while Cwiz was out gardening during class for Mr. M, he got into a minor fender-bender, which caused him to be extremely late. When he got back to the classroom, he sheepishly walked in to return the keys.

Mr. M looked up as Cwiz came to his desk. "Where have you been?"

Cwiz said, "Sorry. I was in a little wreck."

Cwiz turned around and saw the students looking at him. Mr. M gestured to keep his voice down.

Mr. M whispered, "What are you talking about?"

"I had a little accident. I clipped this lady's car in the parking lot in your condo complex."

Mr. M stood up and walked Cwiz out the door, and out of earshot of the kids in class. "Did you call the police?"

"No. I just got her info."

"OK. Give it here."

Cwiz was puzzled. "You want her information?"

Mr. M nodded and held his hand out. Cwiz gave him a little crumpled piece of paper which had the lady's name, driver's license, and phone number.

Mr. M looked very serious and pointed at him. "Don't tell anyone what happened. Got it?"

Cwiz nodded.

"I'll call her up and take care of it. How much do you need to fix your car?"

"I don't know."

"Just get it looked at by a body shop and tell me what it costs, and I'll take care of it."

Cwiz said, "OK. I'm fine by the way."

Mr. M said, "Go home."

Mr. M no doubt realized what hell would rain down on him if Cwiz reported that he was employed by his teacher and working as his gardener off campus when he was supposed to be in class.

Even as a high schooler, Cwiz somehow figured out how to skip class with his teacher's permission, get paid for doing so, pass the class while absent, and have someone else pay for his car accidents.

LIFE LESSON:
It pays to have a side hustle.

Chapter 7

Airport Shenanigans

We made a lot of bad home movies in high school, with a massive handheld video recorder. I know this is probably hard for some of you younger humans to understand, but in those days, you had to record a video on a cassette tape, a big one about 9 inches long, and that cassette tape was physically inserted into an even larger shoebox-sized video recorder, which usually had a huge viewfinder jutting out.

These recording devices were so large and heavy that they were fitted out with a foam pad so that you would not be injured while the video camera rested on your shoulder and your eye was firmly planted in the viewfinder. There were no cell phones then (except that huge one that Michael Douglas's character Gordon Gecko had in the movie *Wall Street*), and certainly not any phones that had photo or video capability.

One day, Cwiz, Reggie, and I decided to go to LAX to videotape some pranks. This was around 1989, when people were still permitted to go all the way into the airport terminals without passing through a security check. We parked in the structure, took our cinder block of a video camera and headed into the terminal looking for some way to cause problems.

There were huge stacked luggage lockers against the wall near the gates in the terminal, and there were people coming and going, waiting for their flights to depart. We decided it would be funny to stuff Cwiz into a luggage locker. Cwiz somehow managed to insert his larger-than-average frame into this tiny locker, including his head, and we closed the door. Reggie started filming.

I pretended that I was trying to open the locker and asked a passerby for help.

I said, "Excuse me, sir, can you help me open this locker? I'm trying to get my bag out and it's stuck."

The man politely obliged, dropped his own bag, and walked over. He turned the latch on the locker door, and Cwiz came springing out of the locker, scaring the bejesus out of the poor guy.

Cwiz and I promptly fell on the ground and held our stomachs, laughing our asses off. The poor man leapt into the air, nearly keeled over from an exploding heart, picked up his bag, and huffed off to eat a Cinnabon or something.

We then did this to roughly 642 more people, to the delight of everyone in the terminal (who were not victims of the prank). It never got old. That is, until airport security rudely interrupted our fun and yanked Cwiz out of the locker, saying, "Hey, you aren't supposed to go in there! What's wrong with you?!"

On another occasion at the airport, Cwiz, me, and a few others whose names escape me were walking outside the terminal near the loading zone where people parked their cars and ran in to meet arriving passengers. Our group walked past a clean and apparently new four-door sedan that was parked in the loading zone. I think it was a Honda Accord. Anyway, its trunk was open and there was not a single thing in it, not a speck of dust. I don't know why, but while walking past, I said, "Hey, Cwiz, you should get in and hide, and we'll freak the dude out when he comes out with his bags."

So, naturally, he did. Cwiz jumped in the trunk, with plenty of room to spare, and I slowly closed the lid as much as I could without latching it.

The rest of our group faded into the background and sort of sulked against the wall, waiting for the sedan's owner to come out. Eventually, a thirtysomething man walked out, dragging two roller bags behind him, and walked up to the trunk. He looked puzzled as he approached, as if thinking, *I know I opened this trunk?*

He walked up, let go of the bags, and opened the trunk lid. Out popped a coiled-up Cwiz with a shriek. The dude jumped back and threw up his hands to protect himself. He was terrified at first, but as the fright faded, a swelling rage came over him.

Cwiz was laughing hard, and the furious man saw the group of us laughing with him. Cwiz started walking away toward us, laughing all the way, when suddenly, the dude started running at us. *Oh crap! Here he comes!*

Cwiz turned around, right in front of another car that was parked and waiting for someone to arrive with bags. The dude rushed Cwiz with a good deal of momentum and shoved him with both hands onto the hood of the other car. Cwiz flew onto the car and rolled sideways with his face toward the windshield. The dude balled his hands into fists and looked ready to throw blows with Cwiz, calling for him to come off the car to fight.

But Cwiz stayed on the hood of the car. Holding his stomach and laughing hysterically, he rolled back and forth. The car hood he was lying on made popping noises as its shape bent and buckled from his weight shifting back and forth. Cwiz's high-pitched laugh threw the dude off guard. The dude watched him laugh for several seconds, looked confused, and then slowly dropped his hands and walked back to his car, shaking his head. When he was gone, we helped Cwiz off the hood and walked off together.

LIFE LESSON:
Laughter will get you out of all sorts of jams.

CHAPTER 8

THE TYCOON

Cwiz did not take the ACT or the SAT in order to gauge his ability to enroll in an elite university, or any college at all. He seemed to know at an early age that he had no interest in college. Evidently, high school had solidified in his mind that he was not interested in the typical academic pathway. He never even signed up to take the tests.

Perhaps what made this so clear to him was that he somehow failed Spanish, while simultaneously being fluent in the language. That must have clued him in to this fundamental truth: not everyone should seek a college degree. The story goes that formal education was not suitable for Einstein, and evidently, it was not suitable for Cwiz either. People are complex, and not everyone listens, learns, and pays attention in the same way. Some people think differently, and Cwiz is clearly one of those people.

For me, after high school, my four-year college plans fell through on account of my dad losing his job the summer after my graduation. As a result of this unplanned financial difficulty, I found myself enrolled in our local community college and started working on general education courses, riveting ones like College Algebra and Art History 100.

Cwiz joined me at the community college. He was taking one course: swimming. I decided to take it with him. On the first day of class, I showed up wearing one of my old Speedos from my high school swim team days. Cwiz showed up wearing baggy turquoise swim trunks with huge pockets.

While we prepared to hop in the pool, I asked him, "What the heck are you wearing?"

He looked down and gestured grandly. "These sexy things here? These are my lucky trunks."

I said, "Look around dude. You're the only one here in lucky trunks. You are gonna die in those things. You need a Speedo."

"I'm not wearing an around-the-hip-wienie-grip. That's not my thing."

"Suit yourself, but you'll be draggin' ass."

Cwiz said, "I'll be fine," as he stretched his arms over his head with a smirk.

I dove in the water, laughing to myself as I did so, knowing this would not go well. Cwiz had never been part of a swim team, and had never taken a swim class. I knew from personal experience that a person's first swim workout usually goes terribly. And sure enough, after fifty yards of Cwiz crawling across the pool with his body at a 45-degree angle, pulling pockets full of water like he was strapped to a parachute, Cwiz reached unsteadily for the wall, pulled his chin into the pool gutter, and yacked up his breakfast.

I stopped at the wall as he rested and whispered to him, "Those trunks *are* sexy."

"Shut up!"

I shot off the wall, giggling bubbles as I went.

After that auspicious start, Cwiz invested in a Speedo, wisely determining that an aerodynamic pelvic section was critical to buoyancy and speed.

So, every other day that semester, we shimmied into our Speedos in the locker room and paraded ourselves out to the pool deck, where we proceeded to hammer our bodies into shape, and mostly, *tried* to flirt with girls (emphasis on the word *tried*). Getting in shape was Cwiz's entire focus at school that semester, and when I asked him whether he intended to take any other courses, he said flatly he was not interested in any of that. I did not pry, wondering what he had in mind for his future.

Cameron, a buddy of ours, told me that around this time, he once had a conversation with Cwiz about what he wanted to do with his life.

Cwiz memorably replied, "I want to be a tycoon."

Cam said, "What does that mean?"

"It means I am going to call my own shots."

Tycoons do not need to sit in Art History 100, nor do they need a solid foundation in English literature. What they need is to know how to hustle. So while I was slowly working my way through equations I will never use in my life, Cwiz was working on his abs, with aspirations of hustling his way into tycoon-hood, where he would be making his own way, on his own terms.

LIFE LESSON:
Know thyself.

CHAPTER 9

PERMANENT RECORD

After Cwiz and I graduated from high school in 1991, we ended up working as security guards together at Fountain Valley High School (FVHS—*Go Barons!*), where we had recently been students.

This guy Barry, who was a high school leader at our church, was a security guard at FVHS when we were still students there. When Barry was leaving the job a few years later, he put in a good word for me and I took over his position. So I started working at FVHS at nineteen years of age, and when a position opened up for another security guy a few months later, I recommended Cwiz.

The school's vice principal (Mr. Christenson) undoubtedly remembered Cwiz as a student, so it was a small miracle that Cwiz was hired. But just like that, Cwiz and I were working together at FVHS, and as security guards. I know. It makes no sense.

One day, while we were "working," which consisted mostly of flirting with the girls we were supposedly protecting with our flimsy walkie-talkies, Mr. Christensen's secretary asked us to throw out a couple of huge garbage bags that were lying in the corner of the office. She told us she was cleaning out the central file cards and that these were from a few years ago, meaning that these files were from our graduating year.

A central file card is a sheet of 8.5 x 11 card stock, lined, folded in half, and kept in special drawers in a file cabinet in the superintendent's office. In those days, each student had one physical central file card that recorded infractions, disciplinary proceedings, detentions, and the like, all written down in one place. In other words, the card was a running log of all a student's sins. No doubt these days such things are computerized, but this was 1993.

For many—indeed most—students, their central file cards were nearly blank. If the student had never shown up late to class, had never had an unexcused absence, was never assigned detention, never suspended, or never in a fight, the card would be completely blank. If a teacher or administrator wanted a shorthand way to check out what kind of student you were, apart from your GPA, this little card would give a snapshot of your record of behavior.

With these garbage bags full of old cards, you can imagine how intrigued we were, knowing that the secrets of our entire graduating class were in our hands. All of our friends' and enemies' dirty deeds were in those bags. We gathered up the bags, found a side room, and started rifling through the cards, looking for anyone we knew.

We quickly found Ian's card. The Captain had a few hiccups here and there, a few detentions maybe, but nothing of major significance. His card had only a few lines on it. It was the same with mine, which we also found quickly. My card was perhaps five percent filled out, and the rest was blank. Ian and I were pretty good students who rarely got into any sort of trouble.

We found other friends' cards. We laughed at their pictures and read the uninteresting comments: *Tardy on X date*; *detention for unexplained absence on X date*.

And then we found Cwiz's card. Jackpot!

This was a different thing altogether. Not only was every line on the card filled out, someone had found it necessary to staple a new sheet to the card in order to fit in all of the damning accusations. When we scanned down the innumerable handwritten entries, we saw numerous detentions, and the usual tardies and absences. Those run-of-the-mill infractions usually took up one line, although there were many, many lines like that on Cwiz's card.

But one entry blew my mind and has stuck with me forever. This intriguing and wordy entry was a full paragraph long, written by Vice Principal Christensen himself in an angry script, with smudged ink, and it went something like this:

Rec'd call from Rm 204 re disruptive student. Victor[1] was brought to my office. We talked about his behavior and the disruption he caused in class for ten minutes. Little remorse. I left Victor in my office to think about his conduct and attended to other matters. When I came back into my office, I sat behind my chair and noticed that he had taped everything to my desk with scotch tape. Victor took the tape off my desk and affixed everything to my desk, including my pencil, my papers, my keyboard, my phone and the pictures of my family. I immediately reprimanded him and called his mother in to pick him up. He thought it was funny. Victor was told not to return to school until tomorrow. One day suspension.

This lovely paragraph tells us a lot about Cwiz. What he did in that office while he waited for Christensen to return was so beautifully pointless, so perfectly funny and harmless. What was going through his head when he decided to do this?

He had just gotten reamed by the main authority figure in the school, the person assigned the task of meting out harsh punishments to students. If you were going to be scared of anyone at our school, it was Mr. Christensen, the dude who had the power to detain you, ruin your Saturdays indefinitely, and suspend or expel you.

After Christensen walked out of his office, leaving Cwiz to sit with his assumed guilt, Cwiz decided the thing to do was not to sit quietly and feign a guilty conscience, but to play a ridiculous prank on the VP. Cwiz knew there was no way Christensen was going to expel him for taping assorted office supplies to his desk. Cwiz knew that deep within his doughy bowels, Christensen would think it was funny, because, of course, it was objectively hilarious.

This is what makes Cwiz so unique. He has always known in his bones what most of us never learn: that the boundaries most people spend their lives worrying about are really an illusion. He

---

1. You are probably wondering, *Who the heck is Victor?* Well, that is Caesar's real name. Weird, right? Like the baby Jesus, he is known by many names.

knew, even then, that these boundaries were always subject to negotiation. It was as if he were constantly asking himself, *Let's see how much I can get away with.*

When you ask yourself that question, over and over again in life, you will find that the world opens up to you in extraordinary ways. And this is especially true if you are pushing the boundaries while making people laugh. This is perhaps Cwiz's most powerful secret.

That is not to say that everyone enjoyed being on the receiving end of Cwiz's experimentation with expected limitations. Sometimes the people who encountered him while he was in his boundary-pushing mode were utterly exasperated.

I'll never forget seeing our exceptionally kind youth pastor, a guy named Bill, completely lose his mind one night when Cwiz was acting up and tell him he was going to kick his ass, in earshot of all of the rest of the high school students at church. I recently asked Bill, who is now the head pastor of the church, about this incident. He said that in the thirty years he has been in ministry, he has lost his cool only twice, and both times, it was because of Cwiz. (Today, Bill is one of Cwiz's closest friends.)

Cwiz could do that to you. I mean, if our mild-mannered pastor Bill could get that pissed, then imagine some rando coming into contact with him in these moments. Some of you reading these early stories of Cwiz's rambunctiousness might be thinking this dude sounds like a jerk. To you I say: stick with me through to the end, because what you'll find is that Cwiz evolves from a sort of annoying prankster to an absolute miracle-worker. The guy whom you may have wanted to punch right in the face becomes the guy you want to wrap in a loving bear hug.

Today, Cwiz is undoubtedly a force for good in the world. Like Aslan in *The Chronicles of Narnia,* he is not safe, but he is good.

LIFE LESSON:
Push the boundaries.

46

PART TWO

ADULTHOOD?

Me and Cwiz meeting David Letterman. (Note that my T-shirt has a picture
of iconic TV character Michael Knight, and Cwiz's proclaims "CWIZ")

CHAPTER 10

FLATBED POOL PARTY

We were bored one day. Really bored.

Often, when it was hot and there was nothing to do, we would end up at the local Thrifty drug store, and we would always get ice cream. Tim was always there. He was a prematurely balding dude in his late thirties who scooped the ice cream, and he'd been scooping and serving punks like us for years. He didn't like us very much.

One day we were harassing Tim for the fiftieth time about whether he could force the brass at Thrifty to come up with a new flavor. We wanted him to call the executives at Thrifty and recommend a chocolate malted crunch and mint chocolate chip mash-up.

Tim stared at us over the rims of his glasses while he scooped. "Do you really think they care what I say?" A long, thin strip of hair came unglued from his scalp and flopped over, swaying while he scooped.

Cwiz said, "Come on, Tim You are gonna own this place someday, dude. You gotta think big!"

Tim sighed and said almost to himself, "You don't know what you're talking about." He handed over the scoop, wiped his sweaty brow with his forearm, and wiped his hands on his pants.

Cwiz was undaunted. "You'll see. Keep your chin up, buddy. See you tomorrow."

On our way back to Cwiz's house, right at the intersection with Thrifty on one side and Baskin-Robbins on the other, we saw a man sitting in a folding chair at the intersection, holding a sign that said, "Will Work for Money." He stared blankly at the world, at nothing in particular, occasionally looking up when someone slowed down next to him. A sedan sidled up to him, rolled down its window, and the driver handed the man a dollar outside the passenger's side window. The man smiled and whispered a thank you.

"We should do that," Cwiz observed.

I said, "What would the sign say?"

Within ten minutes, Cwiz and I were gathering markers and ripping apart a box from Cwiz's trash in order to make signs. We grabbed two beach chairs and an umbrella and drove back to the Thrifty parking lot. It was a hot day, and we knew we would be sweating balls while sitting in the sun on the corner.

When we got to the corner, the man we'd seen was not there. We set up our chairs side by side, right where the other man used to be, and pulled out our signs. One of the signs said "Will Work for Ice Cream" and the other was a dual sign with lettering on both sides of the cardboard. It said "You're Cute" on one side and "Give Me Your Number" on the other.

We took up our spot, and within seconds, we started getting honks. People waved, stared, pointed, and laughed. I held the "Will Work for Ice Cream" sign, and Cwiz held the other sign down on his lap.

When one of the people staring at us happened to be a good-looking girl between the ages of eighteen and thirty, Cwiz would flash the "You're Cute" sign. When he got a positive reception (a giggle or laugh) from the cutie, he would flip the sign over to "Give Me Your Number."

This had been going on for about an hour when a car pulled up behind us. The passenger's door swung open and a woman ran over to us, a single-scooped cone of Thrifty ice cream in each hand, one mint chip and one rainbow sherbet. She handed a cone to each of us. We thanked her as she ran back to her car.

Cwiz said, "I am not eating freekin' sherbert. Gimme that!"

I said, "For the millionth time, it's not sher*BERT*. It's sherbet. No 'R' at the end. It's not a character on *Sesame Street*."

Cwiz held out the colorful cone to me. "You're eating the sher*BERT*."

We switched cones.

We put the signs down and for the next ten minutes, ate our ice cream cones in our beach chairs while the traffic darted around us. When the cones disappeared, the sign went back up and we started over. At some point that day, Cwiz reeled in a phone number.

The success of that little venture morphed into a more elaborate scheme later that week. At the time, Cwiz was driving a Ford F150 truck with an extended bed. Cwiz, the Captain, and I were hanging out one day, again with nothing to do, and decided to go back to the Thrifty parking lot, visit Tim for a scoop, and have a pool party.

We grabbed a giant blue tarp from Cwiz's backyard and put it into the truck bed, tacking it down as best we could. We pulled the truck up on Cwiz's driveway, got out the hose, and filled up the bed with water, which took seemingly forever.

While the pool was filling up, we went to work getting together some pool party toys and snacks. We gathered fun noodles, squirt guns, frisbees, and filled up a cooler with soft drinks and ice.

When we returned to the truck in the driveway, the water had reached the top of the bed, which sagged dangerously low, almost touching the tops of the rear tires. Perfect.

The three of us jumped into the cab and drove very slowly, for less than a mile, to the Thrifty parking lot. The water sloshed violently back and forth the whole time. When the truck came to a stop, the water rushed like a tiny tsunami from the rear of the truck toward the cab, smashing into the window and raining down over the windshield. When Cwiz accelerated, the water ran backward and waterfalled over the back of the bed onto the street. We made it to Thrifty with 75 percent of the flatbed still filled with water. We parked in a corner of the parking lot next to the busy street.

Instant pool party!

Our buddy Chuck drove over to join us, and the four of us took off our shirts and got in the truck's water bed. We made balloon hats and started throwing the frisbee to each other in the pool, even though the pool was only ten or so feet long. We put signs out on the front of the truck advertising the pool party and tried to flag down would-be partygoers to join us. Mind you, this was a Wednesday afternoon.

We heard the usual honks from people going by and saw cars full of people laughing and pointing as they passed by. Taking that as encouragement, we started using our squirt guns to spray the cars as they drove by. A surly dude dressed up like a gangster slowly bicycled by on the sidewalk next to the pool party. Cwiz saw an opportunity and filled up a large syringe-type squirt gun. When the guy got close, Cwiz unloaded a gallon of water on him. The dude ducked but still took the brunt of the blast. He kept riding past us, now soaked, cussing at us as he went. We thought it was the funniest thing we'd ever seen—until he turned back toward us, screaming with menacing hand gestures. I suppose he figured he'd better not take on four dudes at the same time, so he got back on his bike to ride away.

But then he stopped about twenty yards away, dropped his bike, picked up a rock the size of a golf ball, and hucked it at us as hard as he could. It lasered toward us, and we all ducked into the water. The rock slammed the side of the truck's bed, making a loud thwack. Then the guy yelled something about coming back with his friends.

Cwiz inspected the damage, which was minor, and we decided it was probably best to move on. Chuck hopped into his car and drove home. Cwiz got in his truck, and I took the passenger's seat. The Captain stayed in the waterbed and floated freely in the back while we drove him home.

We drove a block toward the Captain's house and wondered what we were going to do with the water. Someone had the brilliant idea of suddenly dumping it on a car behind us if it got too close. We could drop the bed and simultaneously peel out and let the water fly out in spectacular fashion. *Yes*!

We stopped at the next light, where Cwiz intended to make a right turn. We waited until the car behind us, a sedan, got right up against the truck's rear bumper. The light turned green. The Captain floated surreptitiously to the back of the bed, popped up, smiled at the surprised driver directly below him, put his arm over the gate, and flipped the latch.

At the same moment, Cwiz floored it and jerked the wheel right as he made the turn. The Captain lunged for the forward part of the bed as a giant wave of water started pouring out. I looked out of the cab window and saw him floating helplessly out of the bed, riding a wave of inertia over a blue tarp. He looked like Captain Quint in *Jaws* sliding into the shark's mouth at the end of that perfect movie. The Captain was about to body surf a wave that was crashing onto the pavement—the swiftly moving pavement.

Thankfully, the Captain's survival instinct kicked in before he ended up in the street. He made like a starfish, throwing his arms and legs out sideways and propping himself against the bed as the water rushed over him. But the wave was too powerful, and his legs gave way. With his legs dragging on the pavement, he was able to pull himself back into the truck with a Herculean effort.

The massive wave dumped on the car behind us, and as the truck swung around the corner, the wave was thrown sideways all over the street. Hunched over with maniacal laughter, Cwiz and I saw the Captain lying down flat in the bed, now that the water was gone. He stayed that way until we got to his house.

The Captain had a pool at his house, a real one, so when he hopped out of the truck bed, he walked over to the cab and said, "You guys wanna have a pool party here?"

LIFE LESSON:
Don't always go with the flow.

CHAPTER 11

CONCRETE MISSIONARY

Just a year out of high school, in the summer of 1992, Cwiz became a missionary, again. But instead of proselytizing Europe with a wacky group of clowns and puppets, Cwiz decided to go an entirely different route, one that certainly did more to improve people's lives.

During high school, we took trips every year down to Mexico with our church to help build houses for the poor, usually for the week of Spring Break. Our youth group would coordinate with a local ministry whose mission was to build houses for homeless families. We would stay for the week at a local church and work with the church leaders there to do children's ministry and build a small, simple two-room house in one week.

Cwiz was the only one in the group who was fluent in Spanish. He therefore became the guy we all went to for help, and even the adult leaders had to rely on Cwiz to help them communicate with the locals.

It was odd in a way, because Cwiz was universally considered to be the most out-of-control kid in the youth group, the one all the leaders worried about. But in Mexico, forced into a role of responsibility, Cwiz came into his own at the center of the action. He translated directions from the Mexican leadership and told all of us what to do.

Of course, Cwiz had to have some fun with his new role as translator. He told our buddy Cameron, who was studying French in high school, that the Spanish alphabet was the same as the English one, only backwards. That meant the Spanish alphabet started with Z. Cameron tried to work this one out in his brain in the car on the way down.

Then, at the construction site, Cwiz told a huge group of Mexican children that Cameron had candy in his pocket.

"Niños, do you see that tall guy over there with the blond hair? He has pockets full of candy, and whoever catches him first gets it all!"

Cwiz looked at Cam, who was wondering why all the kids were pointing at him. Cwiz said, "Run."

A scream erupted. They chased Cameron around the dirt lot for half an hour, and Cam did not have the slightest idea what was going on.

But most importantly, Cwiz internalized a significant lesson during these short mission trips. He saw first-hand how a family's life could be changed forever by the generosity of others. He spoke with and prayed for these families, who, with tears in their eyes, asked him to translate their gratitude for their new home. We did not understand their words, but we saw them standing in front of their new two-room home, no more than 400 square feet in all, holding each other and beaming with pride. These trips changed Cwiz. He saw how he could help someone, not just with words and promises, but with a foundation, walls, and a roof.

After graduation from high school, Cwiz decided to spend his summer in Mexico. He joined a local mission group called Mexico Inland Mission (MIM). He moved into a house of one of the local missionaries, who provided him with a small room. MIM ministered to a massive settlement of homeless people who scraped together homes from cardboard, plywood, and whatever they could stack together to create a shelter for their families. There were thousands of families there, living in the dirt on the sun-baked hills of the Mexican desert. MIM built homes for these families, one day at a time, one house at a time.

Once Cwiz got down there, he was given the job of pouring concrete foundations for homes that would be built by the youth groups coming in. Every day, he would go to the construction site and mix concrete to get it ready for the foundation pour. Because there was no power source available, the concrete had to be mixed by hand, which was grim work. Imagine mixing thick pancake mix with a shovel in a wheelbarrow for hours on end. This was sweaty toil in the hot sun.

And in order to mix concrete, you need water. The only water source available to them was a river that the village used as a toilet. Cwiz had no choice but to collect this filthy water, try to strain it the best he could to remove maggots and human waste, and then pour it into the dry concrete mix and blend it together. Once the concrete was at the right consistency, they would pour the foundation.

That was just the start of the day. Then Cwiz was off to the border in a car to pick up the youth groups to caravan them to the construction site. After that, he helped supervise the work and act as translator for the groups all day.

Although his work was rewarding, Cwiz felt alone. There was no one his age he could call a friend. None of us were there to joke around with him. As the summer dragged on, he found himself relying more on his faith, finding a friendship with God, and finding happiness by creating it for others.

That summer mission trip had at least three major impacts on his life. First, during that summer, and perhaps most significantly, he learned that he could use his gifts to make a huge difference in people's lives, and he found that he loved doing this for people. He learned that his heart expanded when he did things for others. Simply put, it made him feel good.

Second, that summer revealed to him an interest in construction. This seed of interest, later in life, flowered into a construction license and a thriving construction business.

Third, during that summer, he ate street tacos every night. After the trip, he could never find carne asada like he found there in Mexico, and for years (decades even), he asked himself why no one was making street tacos like that in California. His love of asada tacos was eventually channeled into opening a taco shop in

Fountain Valley when he was in his forties. The restaurant offered wood-fired Tijuana-style tacos—the beloved Tio Flaco's Tacos that many of us now enjoy on a weekly basis.

LIFE LESSON:
When you help someone, you help yourself.

CHAPTER 12

The Valet Days

You should not trust your valet parking attendant. It turns out that many of those dudes, with their black vests and smiling faces, barely know how to drive. And some of them are seriously curious about how fast a Porsche can accelerate off the line. They just never had access to a Porsche, until you showed up and handed them the keys.

For a couple years, Cwiz and I worked for a valet company, along with the Captain, Cory, Amir, and a bunch of our other friends. It was mostly a weekend gig for us. The valet company we worked for had contracts with restaurants, hotels, and, sometimes, individuals throwing private parties. The valet company recruited heavily at Amir's university during his freshman year of college. The word got out, and before long, nearly all of us buddies had been hired as valets.

Cwiz started working for the company, and in a relatively short time, he was promoted to what they called a "door." The "door" was the guy who managed the operation on site, made sure the host was happy, took customer tickets, and managed to keep himself from sweating like the rest of his crew. The "door" was the front door of the operation, so to speak, interfacing with the customers while the valets ran their asses off back and forth from the parking lot, to park or retrieve the cars.

I worked sporadically for the company when I needed some extra money. One of my first jobs was at the Breakers Hotel in Long Beach. Cwiz was the door that night, and some muckety-mucks showed up for the party that was somewhere up on the top floor of the hotel. The smelly valets were not allowed up there.

I was a little nervous about the job, because I had not yet learned how to drive stick. When a slick couple showed up in a Porsche 911 and handed me the keys, I waited by the door for them to go into the hotel. Trying to appear nonchalant, I looked at Cwiz, who was making small talk with the couple. Cwiz knew I was going to have trouble with this one. The couple, apparently suspicious, stayed put, evidently wanting to see me pull away elegantly from the curb.

I gulped, hopped into the bucket seat, and smiled weakly at Cwiz through the passenger's side window. Cwiz bent down so he could see me through the window and gave me a giant, toothy grin that said he could not wait for what was about to happen.

Cwiz said, "Listen. If you give it enough gas, the car will not stall. Just give it plenty of gas, let the clutch out, and you're all good." Cwiz tapped the hood of the car twice and walked back to stand with the car's owners.

That didn't sound too hard. With my left foot on the clutch and my right on the gas, I shifted the car into first gear and pressed down with my right foot. The engine revved up, loud, and started to whine. I looked at Cwiz again and he mouthed the words: "*Pop the clutch!*"

I thought I was letting the clutch out slowly, but it had a mind of its own and popped out forcefully. The tires started spinning and shrieking, and the car shot off the curb like a bullet. I jerked the wheel left and spun around the circular driveway at the front of the hotel, bounced onto the street with a bang, and instantly made a right turn down the hill to the parking lot behind the hotel.

In front of the hotel, as a rubbery smoke cloud wafted away, the owners were pissed. "What the hell was that?"

Cwiz said, "Sorry about that. I'll have a word with him when he gets back up here."

"He can't do that!"

"Of course you're right, sir. I think he was a little too anxious to get to the next guest. We've got a line forming here. But I'll make sure he doesn't do that again. I apologize."

When I got back to the front of the hotel, Cwiz asked me if I would go get us all some McDonald's.

"Should I take the Porsche?"

"Of course. You need the practice, right?"

I ran back to the Porsche to get our dinner.

Because Cwiz worked for the company for so long, and because he often had to lug the company's equipment around, his garage started to fill up with company property. He had a big, free-standing steel sign that he would set up in front of the party, which said "VALET" on it and contained our "terms and conditions," which basically said if we drove your car off a cliff, or into a bus full of children, it was your fault, you would be paying for it, and you would likely face criminal prosecution. He also had boxes of those little tickets that tear in two, which also contained the "terms and conditions," and a keyboard, which was a board with pegs on it to hang the keys.

Cwiz would sometimes get a call at the last minute to handle a job. He would load up his car, put on his clip-on bow tie, and head out. The Captain and I would often receive those last-minute calls from him, asking us to tag along. After the initial rush, when all the partygoers were inside enjoying themselves, Cwiz would make his way into the party and come out with three plates full of munchies. Then he would regale us with promises of the tip he was going to pull down for us that night.

"You guys are working hard out here, man. I'm gonna hook you guys up tonight."

Then, at the end of the party, Cwiz would tell the owner of the home how hard we had been working, emphasizing the rugged topography of the neighborhood.

"You know these guys had to park on the next block, down that hill? They have been running up and down that hill all night! Anything you can do to help them out for the hard work would be great."

He would come back with $100 or $200 extra in tips, which we would split equally before it was added on to the tips we made from each individual car we brought in. There was not a door in the company better than Cwiz at landing large personal tips.

After watching the valet company prosper first-hand, and learning how the company worked, Cwiz realized he could do this on his own. He went to a Kinko's and copied up some cheesy fliers that said "Chezerray Valet." He put his home phone number on the flyer and asked Cory to help him pass out fliers in some ritzy neighborhoods in Newport Beach, including Balboa Island, where parking was tight. When Cory balked, Cwiz said he would give him 30 percent of any profits the company made.

They spent a day passing out the cheesy fliers. Nobody called. But then, four years later, the phone rang.

Cwiz answered, "Hello."

"Um, hi. Is this Chezerray Valet?"

Without missing a beat, Cwiz said, "Yep, sure is."

"Hi, I have a party coming up at my house and I need valet."

"No problem. When is the party?"

Cwiz had not worked as a valet in over three years, but his garage still held the equipment. He dusted off the old stuff, and Chezerray Valet worked its one and only job on Balboa Island, using the other company's signs, keyboard, and tickets. Cory pocketed 30 percent of the job.

LIFE LESSON:
When opportunity calls, spring into action.

CHAPTER 13

PAINT GUN ATTACK

For a few years, from the age of about eighteen to twenty-one, our group of buddies took great delight in shooting each other in the face with paintball guns. We started off slow with paint gun play, as anyone does with a new hobby. We dipped our toes into this underworld where weekend warriors, off-duty cops, retired military members, and everyday morons like us got together to shoot each other with tiny projectiles. We all bought the cheapest guns possible at first. The first guns we had were pistols called "Splatmasters," which held a single tube of ten paintballs and required frequent air cartridge changes.

The first night we went out to play, we went to an empty field in Fountain Valley in the middle of the night and tried to shoot each other through the fog. We donned flexible plastic shop goggles from Home Depot and lay in the dirt with our Splatmasters at the ready, each of us afraid to be the first to get shot, having no idea what it would feel like. Our goggles fogged up, nobody got hit, and it was generally considered a bust.

After that lame beginning, we decided we needed somewhere cool to play, someplace out of the way, someplace with hiding spots, nooks and crannies. So we waited again until late at night and drove over to an elementary school. We split up into teams and spread out across the school. We spent the night shooting the place up and having a fantastic time.

We learned that night that a tiny, semi-hard ball traveling at nearly 200 feet per second could hurt like a mamma jamma, depending on how close you were to the shooter when you were shot. We also learned you did not want to get shot in the face. At one point, Cwizzy took a shot while peering over a ledge down at Cory, who pointed up and shot Cwiz right between his front tooth and his upper lip. The lip swelled up like a fat sausage under his nose. So, before long, we all had real goggles, with attachable face masks.

Then there was an arms race. Cliff somehow scored an unholy cannon, which was clearly not street legal. It was a pump-action rifle and could hold over 150 balls with a gravity-fed top loader. When Cliffy shot the thing, it sounded like a freakin' Howitzer and you could hear the ball screaming over your head as it peeled back the air in front of it. It scared the hell out of us pistol-toting losers, and Cliffy suddenly became Enemy No. 1. It didn't help that Cliffy walked around with a puffy life vest that literally deflected paint balls and fired them back at you. He was like a paintball supervillain, laughing maniacally as he hunted us. As you might imagine, we all showed up at our next outing with semi-automatic rifles purchased on new credit cards, hoping to compete with him. Over time, we became seasoned players, with a host of wounds and bruises to prove it.

During this same time frame as our paintball days, we were in an ongoing prank war with a group of girls at the church. I have no idea how the pranks started, but someone started them, and they were now a weekly back and forth occurrence between the church dudes and the church girls. The pranks were getting worse as time went on.

After returning from a paintball outing with the boys one day, Cwiz and I went out to the church parking lot where we had left our cars and found that the girls had defiled them again. Each car had been carefully covered with feminine products, evenly spaced over the windshields and windows. Even the side mirrors were defiled. We didn't even know what these sticky things were that clung to our car's every inch, but we knew this required a forceful response. No claim of responsibility was needed.

The girls always seemed to attack our cars when we went on our paintball excursions, because all of us guys met up at the church to carpool together. Just a week or so before, we arrived at the church to find our cars stickered bumper to bumper with Double Stuf Oreos. The girls split them in half and stuck them, frosting side down, all over our cars. I figured the girls must have eaten the non-sticky halves. I hope they had milk.

Looking back, I wonder at all the time we had. We were always together in those days. We were all out of high school and going to regular college group meetings probably two or three times a week in various formats. None of us seemed to be doing anything else. We all had part-time (very part-time) jobs, in some cases several different very part-time jobs, and college classes were sporadic, for the most part. Cwiz and I were in our swimming class together at the community college but seemed to be doing little else.

With all the time on our hands, we were always looking for trouble. It should probably be clear by this point, but "trouble" for us was different than it was for most people our age. We were committed Christians. We did not drink, do drugs, or have sex (as far as I know, anyway). So we had to be far more creative than others to get our giggles. We got off by screwing around with people, doing oddball things in public, and playing these pranks on each other.

On a Friday night shortly after the panty-liner incident, which was not long after the Oreo attack, a ridiculous and amateurish toilet-papering took place at Cwiz's house. He came out on Saturday morning to find long strings of toilet paper waving from the shrubs in front of his house and tumbleweeding down the street in the wind. He was not amused.

When several of us showed up at Cwiz's house later that day to pick him up for paintball, he showed us the annoying shards of TP that were impossible to remove in the trees and shrubs in front of the house. As the Dude from *The Big Lebowski* would say, "This aggression will not stand, man." The ball was definitely in our court to attack, and we discussed various options, never settling on the best responsive prank. Instead, we all went paintballing again and were gone all day.

As luck would have it, we happened upon Tiffany (one of the girls who was involved in the pranks) in her car that night driving home. We were tired from our game, still donning our combat fatigues and aching from several welts recently inflicted on us from too close a range. It was late at night, and Fountain Valley's streets were emptying out. Cory and I were in his old Honda Accord, with Cwiz in the back seat. Cliffy was following us in his car with the Captain. We came to a stop at a light, and lo and behold, Tiffany was sitting at the light next to us, clueless that we were there and that we had several loaded paint guns on hand.

We figured it was as good a time as any to retaliate.

Cory pulled up next to her with her car on his driver's side. She looked forward with a blank stare, waiting for the light to change. I rolled down my window and climbed out, put my butt on the window sill, put my left hand on the inside roof handle for safety, and extended my right arm over the roof of our car, with the rifle pointed toward her car. I pointed it right at her, but her passenger's side window was up. Cwiz, from the back seat driver's side window, pointed his gun at her car too.

The light turned green. She looked over and saw the guns pointed at her, we heard a muffled scream, and she took off. Cory stomped on the gas and gave chase. Cwiz and I started firing.

Clack, clack, clack, clack, clack.

The paintballs splattered in mini technicolor fireworks on her side windows. She swerved and tried to get in front of us, but Cory would not let that happen. He sped up to keep pace, and we continued firing.

As the chase continued, paint splattered all over her windows, fenders, and hood. It ricocheted off the back window, the neon paint of pink, green, and blue running down the car in streaks.

At one point, she slammed on her brakes, flipped a quick U-turn, and again jammed her foot on the gas. Cory followed suit in a screaming left U-turn from the far-right lane. My body nearly flew out of the car, but I hung on to the handle and kept firing. I could hear Cwiz hooting from the back, over the sounds of roaring engines, screeching tires, wind in my ears, and clacking paintball guns.

Tiffany did her best to lose us, but it was never going to happen with Cory—a demon in his old Honda—at the wheel. He knew that car like his own body.

As an aside, Cory was known to turn the Honda's ignition off while driving and pull the key out while the car coasted down the freeway in neutral. While the car sped along with no power, he used the car key to pry a stuck cassette tape out of the stereo, flipped the cassette tape, put it back in the stereo, stuck the key back in the car, turned the car back on, threw it back in gear, and proceeded down the freeway as if it was nothing. Mind you, all of this was done in a single fluid, lightning-fast motion. Like I said, Cory was a demon driver with mad skills. That is to say, Tiffany's old Ford Escort was never going to get out of our gun sights.

Cliff and the Captain trailed behind us in Cliffy's red GMC Jimmy but managed to stay close and watch the whole thing unfold. I looked back to give Cliff and the Captain the thumbs up, laughing heartily, but suddenly Cliffy hit the brakes and made a hard left turn out of view down a side road.

I could not figure out why Cliffy took off. I shrugged and kept firing at Tiffany's now tie-dyed car. Tiffany headed toward her house in North Huntington Beach, and for a full ten minutes, we continued pelting the car. It was entirely covered, and even at stop lights, we continued firing. *Reload!*

She turned left, and left again, into her neighborhood. As we followed her, and as I continued firing out the window over the hood of the Honda into her back window, I saw the immediate area around our car suddenly light up. I looked up and saw, and then heard, a helicopter, masked by a blinding light directly overhead.

I squirmed back into the car, and said, "Holy crap, guys! Cops!"

Cwiz quickly looked back and said, "Dude, that is not Cliffy behind us, that's the po-po."

Then, as if perfectly choreographed, the neighborhood was blocked off, with cop cars appearing in every conceivable direction in an instant. One pulled in front of Tiffany's car, and she slammed on her brakes. Two more came from the sides, and a police cruiser closed off the route behind us, as Cory too shrieked to a stop. An abrupt cacophony of mechanical noise erupted—helicopter wash and thumping overhead. Angry police officers screamed at us to raise our hands. Six hands shot straight up out of the car windows.

Cory, Cwiz, and I stared at each other in disbelief. Our eyes drifted to the several guns on the back seat, and without saying a word to each other, we knew we were royally screwed.

One by one, we were ordered out of the car by a loud, gruff voice whose owner was obscured by several spotlights. We walked backwards, hands erect, and lay face down on the street, the three of us next to each other. The cops closed in, pulled our paint guns out of the car, laid them on the trunk of the Honda, and eventually asked us to sit on the curb.

They talked to Tiffany first. We watched her talk to them while we sat on the curb, wondering whether she was going to get her ultimate revenge right now. She could say she didn't know who we were, that we were terrorizing her, and she wanted to press charges. The tables had turned, in epic fashion. She seemed gleeful while she looked at us sitting there. We could tell she was turning the matter over in her mind.

But while they were speaking, I saw two other officers inspecting our paint guns and starting to laugh. The levity between them told me we were going to be okay. One of the cops walked over to us and looked at us. We were still wearing our camouflage clothes.

"What are you guys doing here tonight?"

I said, "We were playing paintball in Aliso Viejo, and then…." I trailed off.

The cop said, "And then what?"

"Well, we saw our friend. We know her, and it was sort of a prank revenge thing."

"So you started shooting her car and chasing her all over the city."

"Something like that."

"Where exactly were you guys playing paintball?"

"Aliso Canyon."

"I haven't played there. Is there an actual facility there or just open space?"

"No, we just found an open area there."

"That's good. I've got the same gun as one of you."

"Really? You play?"

"Yeah, little bit." The cop smiled. He said, "Listen, guys, we're gonna take it easy on you tonight, but you should realize how bad this could have gone for you."

We started spilling all over ourselves to thank him.

"But hey, here's what you're going to do. You're all going to her house right now, and you're going to wash the paint off her car. In fact, you're going to make her car look brand spankin' new. You got it?"

"Yes, sir."

Tiffany's house was just a street over. We pulled her car up into her driveway, pulled the hose out of the dark bushes, found some sponges in her garage, and washed her car. Tiffany looked on with smug delight, laughing while she called the other girls to tell them what happened, gloating the entire time.

LIFE LESSON:

When the tables turn on your enemy, be magnanimous in victory.

CHAPTER **14**

THE KIDNAPPING

Cliffy was driving. His red 1991 GMC Jimmy was gaining speed through the housing tract as he stomped on the gas. I was in the passenger's seat, white-knuckling the overhead handle as we hung a hard right around a quiet corner of the dark street. Cwiz was in the back with pantyhose on his head, shouting at Joann, who was curled up in the rear compartment area, playing along with our little stunt. The Captain was also yelling incoherently, generally whooping it up for the feat we had just pulled off. Amir was in the middle seat, exuberantly asking us, "Did you see their faces? Did you see that?"

We had just (sort of) kidnapped Reggie's sister, Joann, from their house during a Bible study in their living room. Don't be alarmed. No one called the police, and everyone involved knew it was all in good fun. But the mission, and its execution, was nothing short of a masterpiece. SEAL Team Six could not have done better.

Here's what happened: We knew that Reggie was having a Bible study at his house that night, and that approximately a dozen people would be gathered in his living room, and that they would be singing while Reg played the guitar. We had been to his house many times, so we knew the layout.

For some unknown reason lost to history, we decided we would raid the house and steal one of the people there. It didn't matter which one we took. And then we would demand something from the group in order to return the person. But we could not figure out anything we wanted from Reg, so we dropped that part and decided we would just kidnap somebody for an hour or so.

You might be wondering why. What was the point? The truth is I have no idea. We had gotten into our heads for some reason that this would be a fun thing to do to Reggie during his little Bible study, so...

We gathered the following gear:

- Headset (hands-free) walkie-talkies
- Black clothes from head to toe
- Pantyhose
- Rope
- Duct tape
- Paint guns
- Mexican fireworks and rocket boxes left over from the Fourth of July
- Sock bombs
- Doritos

Cwizzy, Cliffy, the Captain, Amir, and I piled into the Jimmy and made the two-block drive from Cwiz's house to Reg's house. We noted the familiar cars piled up around Reggie's driveway. The usual suspects were all there.

We double-parked directly in front of the house. We would not be long. As we piled out, Cliff opened the trunk to receive the incoming human cargo and began assembling the fireworks on the sidewalk out front, just twenty-five feet from Reg's front door.

The Captain and I ran to the side gate and checked the latch. It was open, so we would not have to climb the fence. Amir and Cwiz assembled at the front door. It was unlocked. They waited for the go-ahead on the headset radio, then the Captain and I snuck down the side yard. Reggie did not have a dog, so no concern there. We found the electrical panel and opened it up. We could hear soft singing coming through the sliding glass door just a few feet away from us.

I said over the walkie-talkie, "We're cutting power on 3, 2, 1. Blackout."

The Captain pulled the switch and instantly, the entire house went black. The singing stopped.

I said quietly into the headset, "Go!"

At the signal, Cwiz and Amir barged into the house, went directly into the living room, which was pitch black, and grabbed the first person they could. Four hands grabbed unknown limbs and hauled a female person out of the living room. It happened to be Reg's sister, Joann.

While they were grabbing their victim, the Captain and I ran as fast as we could back to the front door. As we passed the garage, we saw Cliffy light up the fireworks and then jump into the driver's seat. We got to the front door as the guys carried Joann to the car and put her into the trunk. She went along with the game.

Joann was laughing and said, "Caesar, what are you guys doing? What is going on? Where are we going?"

Cliffy yelled out, "Shut it and do what you're told."

Cwizzy shushed Cliffy and said quietly to her, "Just play along. We're just going to my house."

Before the trunk shut, she fake yelled out to her friends, "Help!"

The Captain and I, as the plan called for, were at the door ready for people to come spilling out of the house to rescue the victim. But we were armed with what we called "sock bombs," which were designed to stymie any attempted rescue.

The bombs were nothing more than tube socks filled with all-purpose flour. My guess is the manufacturers of the flour had not counted on this particular purpose for their product. We strangled the tops of the tube socks to keep the flour from spilling out, and the socks hung down a full foot long, heavy in our hands, as big as a tube of tennis balls.

With Joann in the trunk, as the rockets began firing into the sky behind us, Reg and Sean came running out to save her, with Heather following behind them. But, as they exited the house, they did not see the Captain and me. All they could see was a fantastical fireworks display unlike anything Reggie's street had ever seen.

Thanks to Cliffy's Mexican fireworks, hundreds of bottle rockets were firing from Reggie's front lawn far into the air and exploding with deafening booms. As soon as they came out onto the porch, their eyes immediately went up to the sky and their mouths opened. Reggie looked up in awe straight over our heads, with the rocket blasts reflecting from his large, thick glasses.

While they were admiring the rocket show, the Captain and I reversed our holds on our sock bombs, held them by the toe with the open end up, and swung the tube socks right at them in a large circular throwing motion. The sock bombs exploded on Sean and Heather, who were now blinded by a deluge of all-purpose flour. A massive white cloud enveloped the entire porch and foyer and wafted slowly into the house.

We turned and ran, and as we did, I could see that Sean and Heather were completely covered head to toe in flour, their faces caked with it. They bent over hacking to get the flour out of their mouths. Like disappearing ninjas in a cloud of smoke, we ran to the car, and Cliffy stomped on it as soon as our butts hit the seats.

Amir said, "Did you see their faces? Did you see that?"

We laughed like insane persons back to Cwiz's house, which took about three minutes. Joann, not even sure what was so funny, laughed right along with us.

As soon as we got there, we got a call from Reg. Joann was sitting in Cwiz's kitchen drinking a Coke and eating Doritos. Reg claimed Heather had to go to the hospital because the flour had expanded in her lungs and she was "literally dying, you guys."

We didn't fall for it.

We told him we'd return Joann after she finished her Coke. No ransom necessary. The memory of a mission accomplished was payment enough.

LIFE LESSON:
Do not overlook the other purposes for all-purpose flour.

CHAPTER 15

THE SCOTT HEAD

For a while, the prank war with the girls got out of hand. Cwiz and I put an advertisement for free purebred golden retriever puppies in the paper with Tiffany's home number. Her answering machine worked overtime on that one. She was pretty pissed.

After the girls retaliated by somehow filling up Cwiz's truck bed with Jell-O (which I must admit was a solid prank), we followed up with garage sale signs at her house and all over her neighborhood, telling the public there was more for sale in the backyard, and to just head on back. We propped open the side gate to make it more inviting. Tiffany woke up on a Saturday morning to strangers milling about her backyard, lifting up potted plants looking for price tags.

But eventually, the pranks tapered off in a fragile cease-fire with the girls, and we directed our substantial time and energies elsewhere, at new targets. And when you are a part of a church with a youth group, and youth leaders who invite you to their homes, and give you nearly unlimited opportunities to mess with them, it is easy to find a new target. Poor Scott, our college pastor, became our target for a time. We did a lot of things to Scott, and none of it was deserved. But some of it was very funny—to us, anyway.

One day, we went to his house unannounced. Cwiz and I rang the doorbell. While we distracted him, Cory snuck through a back door and tried to steal his television. We figured if we could pull it off, it would baffle Scott and his wife Candy for the rest of their lives. They would say, "How did our TV just disappear?" While Cory was trying to get the TV, Candy came walking out in her bathrobe, saw Cory, and screamed. Cory jetted out the back slider and leaped over the back fence. Scott was confused as to what the hell we were doing, and we never let on.

Another time, we went to his house, pulled out his hose from behind his front bushes, and turned it on. One of us rang the door-bell, and when Scott answered the door, the other jumped out of the bushes and hosed him down while he stood in his doorway. Just brutal. (Notice I do not want to say who did what.) He should have kicked our butts for that one.

And then there was the prank known simply as "the Scott Head." Cwiz, the Captain, Sean, and I were hired by the church to stay there overnight to babysit Christmas trees. Yes, that is a thing. The church was holding a fundraiser by selling Christmas trees, so they ordered a huge mess of trees, which were delivered to the church parking lot. The church needed someone to stay overnight to prevent theft, so they hired us four knuckleheads to do it, and they gave us the church keys so that we could sleep in the college room.

About midnight, we were bored. We used the keys they gave us to get into Scott's office and then started thinking of ways we could terrorize him. We looked through his desk and found a picture of his smiling mug. He was goofing off in the photo, and his expression struck us as hilarious. We decided it needed to be memorialized in a big way. So we blew the picture up onto a transparency sheet for an overhead projector and then projected the picture onto a blank wall in the college room. We found some paint and brushes and started carefully tracing Scott's head directly onto the wall.

The head was a full six or seven feet tall and six or so feet wide. It was huge, and it took up the entire formerly blank white wall of the college room. We spent hours painstakingly painting his giant, smiling head on the wall. When it was done in the small hours of the morning, it was perfect. We added an afro for fun.

And because Scott always used to say, "Hey, Lamer," when he saw you, Cwizzy insisted that Scott's head should be saying,

Our masterpiece.

"Hey, Lamer." Instead of painting "Hey, Lamer," we raided the letters we needed from construction paper letters already hanging on the wall to proclaim Jesus's Great Commission.

It was gorgeous.

We vowed, no matter what, and no matter how obvious it was that we were the ones who had done it, we would never, ever admit it (until now, I guess). The next day, at church, some of the leadership was apoplectic. Various reprimands were being thrown around. Discussions were had about the consequences of defacing church property and about the lack of respect for the leadership and maybe even for God. We stayed quiet and privately cherished the Scott Head. Objectively, they had to admit it was pretty good, right? Well, no, it seemed everyone was pissed.

But the Captain, being an Eagle Scout and all, quietly went back to the church a day or so later and painted over the Scott Head, restoring the premises to the status quo. We said no more about it, and no official responsibility was ever taken for the prank. Thankfully, we have a picture and a video recording of the process to remember it.

LIFE LESSON:
If bad pictures of you exist, destroy them immediately.

CHAPTER 16

Never More Happy

There were times when our small team of accomplished pranksters turned on one other. It did not happen often, but if one of our buddies did something to upset the rest of the group, he was going to have to pay the consequences. And the results of these cannibalistic pranks were often spectacular.

Around 1993, several of us guys at the church used to meet up every week in a "small group." It was basically an accountability group, to ensure that each of us was maintaining our faith or keeping the commitments we had each made to God and to each other. Cwiz, the Captain, Amir, Cory, and I had been meeting together for years, since our sophomore year of high school. We continued to meet through our early college years, and others joined from time to time, including Cameron, Chad, and Cliffy. (Evidently, your name had to start with a "C.")

But at some point in 1993, the Captain abruptly stopped coming to our small group, without explanation. When we asked him what he was doing and why he was not showing up, he was coy, dodging our questions. Having known the Captain since I was ten years old, I knew something was up. Cwiz and I decided we needed to get to the bottom of it.

On a day and time that I knew the Captain would not be home, I called his house hoping to obtain information from his family, with whom I was very close.

"Hello?" asked Fiona, Ian's older sister.

"Hey, Fi, it's Jeremy."

"Hey, Jer."

"Is Ian around?"

"No, he's out somewhere right now, not sure where."

"Oh, bummer, okay. I was going to ask him if he was coming to small group tonight. Can you leave him a message to let me know?"

"Tonight? No, he's coming with me and Mom to a class."

"A class? What kind?"

"It's an exercise class."

"Really? What kind of exercise?"

"It's a step aerobics class."

"Oh, cool," I said, stifling a giggle. "Where's the class?"

"It's at the Golden West community center."

"Okay, I'll just check in with him later. Have fun."

"Okay, talk to you later," Fi said.

One millisecond after hanging up, I dialed Cwizzy.

"Dude," I said ominously.

"What?"

"Dude."

"What!?"

"Just pick me up. We have to act fast."

Cwiz came over without another word and picked me up. I told him what was going on, and we quickly went to Reggie's house and picked up his dad's shoebox-sized video camera, the same one we used for the airport locker pranks. We then called the community center and confirmed the time and location of the step aerobics class.

We showed up fifteen minutes ahead of the class start time and rolled up unobtrusively in our car, away from the parking lot, scoping the place out and hoping the Captain would not see us. Soon enough, he pulled up with his mom and sister. He was wearing shorts and a red tank top. Perfect.

In an amazing stroke of luck, the Captain took up a spot in the classroom in the back, right next to an open door that faced the parking lot. No doubt he took the spot in the back because he was afraid he would look like an idiot if he were in front and did not know the steps. The stars were aligning perfectly. It was scrumptious.

When the class started, Cwiz and I army-crawled like trained soldiers behind a tree about 25 feet away from the open door. We pressed record and trained the heavy camera on the Captain's back, and he stepped on the tiny stair in front of him and kicked his right knee in the air, again and again. *Hi-yah!*

The rest of the class in front of him, all women in bright multi-colored leotards, did the same thing. Then they changed legs and knee-kicked again on the other side. Eventually, at the right time in the song, and at the instructor's direction, they spun around on the little plastic stair in a complicated multi-stepped move.

Every time the Captain would spin, he would briefly face outside (at us), and we would have to duck back behind the tree. We would wait a beat, and the camera would come out from behind the tree again, just in time to catch the Captain missing another step. His mom and sister could be seen in front of him, perfectly aligned with the instructor's movements.

We could hardly believe our luck, and we were giggling and grabbing each other as we filmed Ian trying to keep up with the leotarded ladies in his class. My constant laughter rocked and jiggled the camera, and the footage unfortunately suffered for it. Cwiz was laughing so hysterically that he could hardly move. It was almost as if someone had fired a stun gun into him and he was being electrocuted. He lay on the grass behind the tree while I filmed, paralyzed and shaking with ecstatic glee. Tears were in his eyes, and he kept saying, "He's doing spins. He's doing spins." Cwiz had never been happier.

After about fifteen minutes, we figured we had enough material and we snuck off, backing out the way we came. We laughed all the way back to the church, where we quickly got to work editing the footage, overlaying the music, and talking to Dan (our college leader at the time) about what we had done. We put a plan together for the video's best and highest use. This kind of material could not be squandered. It would have to be used to its full potential.

A few nights later, the whole college group assembled in the large youth room for our weekly meeting. There were about forty or so college students there, and the Captain took his place in the crowd, leaning back in a folding chair next to me and Cwiz.

Dan took the stage and announced we had a special video to show the group to start the night. I looked at the Captain, who was sitting next to me, and he had a pleasant non-committal look on his face, curious as to what the video was about.

The video faded in with Dan sitting cross-legged in a leather chair in his office, a Bible in his lap and a bookcase behind him. Dan looked directly into the camera and gravely explained the importance of small groups, how they were designed to establish relationships and maintain a sense of accountability with the group members.

Dan then explained that "sadly," some within our community had decided to forego small groups for other less important endeavors. Dan then looked menacingly at the camera. "This is their consequence."

The scene cut from Dan in his office, and the song "Stayin' Alive" by the Bee Gees kicked in. The screen then faded in, to a tank-topped dude in tight shorts doing knee kicks in a step aerobics class.

I looked at the Captain. His eyes bugged out, and his mouth dropped open. Then he looked at me and Cwiz, hugging each other and wiping tears from our eyes.

As the Captain kicked and gyrated on screen with all of the ladies in the class in the background, Dan's voice could be heard over the Bee Gees disco beats. Dan said, "Not only are small groups critical to building accountability among the members, they are also good for developing other skills and traits, such as rhythm, timing, sense of fashion, and social understanding."

I looked again at the Captain. He dropped his head and shook it slowly as the entire crowd of students turned to look at him. He looked at Cwiz and me and said, "Well done, guys."

LIFE LESSON:
Friends don't let friends jazzercise.

CHAPTER 17

THE FUNNIEST DUDE IN THE ROOM

O nce a year, just like when we were in high school, we would go to a summer camp with our church. But now we were officially adults; this was a camp for college kids, and it was therefore even more difficult for the leaders to tell us to go to bed, to shut up, or to stop harassing the other campers.

Cwiz had come into his own after high school. He was no longer the chubby bando, and because he was usually the funniest guy in the room, the girls liked him. He worked hard at making sure people knew he would "bring the funny," so if there were a couple hundred college students at camp that Cwiz didn't know, he went right to work on night one to make sure they knew who he was.

I recall one camp where college students were slowly filing into the chapel before the evening Bible study. The worship band had finished their warm-ups, and the instruments and microphones were all set up on the stage waiting to be used. Background music played as people chatted and took their seats in the padded pews. To Cwiz, this was an opportunity to make his mark. He walked up and took the stage, then stood behind the microphone and quietly looked at the audience. I watched him, not knowing what he was going to say.

But he didn't *say* anything. Instead, to my surprise, he started to sing. And he can't sing. He really has no talent in that area. But sing he did, at the top of his lungs, and in a high feminine voice. His song had no words. It was just an operatic melody of sorts. He undulated the word *"Ohhhhhhhhhhh"* in an original melody he was creating on the spot. This went on for, no exaggeration here, a full ten minutes. Just the *"Ohhhhh, ohhhh, ohhhh"* like he was a talentless woman shrieking at the opera.

The people from the other churches were confused and looked around at each other for answers. Our group, who knew Cwiz, was dying. I recognized two of the girls in the chapel who had already had a flirtatious conversation with Cwiz. They were both giggling. That was all he was trying to do, and I thought to myself, *mission accomplished*. He ended his "song" with a cacophonous climactic cringey high note. He took a short bow, stepped off the stage, and sat down next to me.

It was an Andy Kaufman-like performance. We low-fived sitting in our chairs. The worship leader took the stage and said blandly as he strapped on his guitar, "Well, thank you for that performance, whoever you are. Now are you guys ready to worship the Lord or what?!"

That weekend, Cwiz was terrorizing everyone there, to the gleeful delight of the rest of us. On Saturday afternoon, everyone was in a session that included singing and sermonizing—the usual church stuff. Session broke, and we had fifteen minutes or so before we needed to be back in the service. Naturally, everyone used the time to head to the bathroom.

When I walked into the men's room with Cwiz, he darted into a stall. I did my thing at the urinal and then went to the sink to wash my hands. In front of me was a mirror, and when I looked in it, I could see Cwiz's head pop up over the top of the stall. He was standing on the toilet, looking over the stall door at me and laughing quietly. He put his finger to his lips to tell me to be quiet.

I turned around and lifted my hands in a questioning manner, to mean, *What are you doing?*

Cwiz pointed to the stall next to him and I could see two large sneakered feet pointing toward me in the stall next to Cwiz. Someone was doing his business.

Cwiz then held up a large roll of toilet paper above the stall door. With an expression of concentration, he stuck his arms over the other stall with the TP in his hands and started unfurling the roll on top of the guy. It was quiet for several seconds, way too long given that the guy must have been completely bewildered as to what was going on.

I could see the two big sneakers shift a little bit, and then he said, "Um, I'm good."

I lost it, and although I tried to muffle my guffaw, the guy heard me, and now he knew someone was screwing with him. Cwiz just kept unrolling it on top of him, and the roll was now halfway gone. I could see it pooling around the guy's feet.

The dude was pissed now.

"Hey! What do you think you're doing?!"

Cwiz said nothing. The TP continued to rain down.

"Hey!"

Cwiz said nothing.

"Stop it right now!"

No words, only TP.

"Okay, then. Here comes the ass-kicking!" The toilet flushed.

Cwiz dropped the tiny remainder of TP on the guy's head and took off out of the bathroom, with me behind him. We were laughing while running for our lives and looking for a place to hide. I ran into the main session room and tried to look natural, as Cwiz ran outside toward a bunkhouse, where he managed to wedge himself under a crawlspace.

From the window in the main room, I could barely see Cwiz's face from behind a grate under the bunkhouse when the victim came flying out of the bathroom, looking left and right.

He was a big dude, and it was a good thing Cwiz got out of there when he did, because he looked ready to kill somebody. He stalked around and eventually gave up. After all, he did not even know who he was looking for. We laughed all weekend every time we saw him.

On another occasion, years later, I was in a men's room again with Cwiz. And once again, I went to the urinal and Cwizzy went into the stall next to some poor unsuspecting dude in the stall going about his business. While I peed, I heard Cwiz latch the stall door and sit down. I knew he wasn't going to the bathroom but was planning on doing something to his unknown stall neighbor. He waited a bit. When I was done peeing, I went to the sink to wash up.

It was really quiet for a beat. Then I heard a soft knock. Cwiz was knocking on the stall next to him. There was no response.

Cwiz knocked again.

Again, Cwiz's stall neighbor was silent.

Cwiz knocked another time.

Then a meek voice said, "No, thank you."

LIFE LESSON:
Never waste good toilet paper.

Chapter 18

Stop Hugging the Guests

Disneyland bills itself as the happiest place on Earth. But if that were true, why do they get pissed when you pass out free hugs to the guests?

Several of us had obtained Disneyland annual passes, which meant we could go to the park whenever we wanted, and we got our money's worth. We quickly got bored with the rides and the lines and started looking for creative ways to have a good time with the guests.

Disneyland has this outdoor theatrical performance and light show called *Fantasmic!* that draws absolutely massive crowds. I'm talking thousands and thousands of people, shoulder to shoulder. Imagine three football fields full of people with not a hair's breadth between them. When the show ends, all of these people funnel through narrow exits in a waddling cluster, all of them anxious to get out of there.

We figured that if we posted up at the exit's bottleneck, we could make everyone feel better by hugging them. Cwiz, some other dudes, and I stood right in the middle of this onslaught of people marching toward us, held our arms out, and started hugging them.

One confused tourist after another stopped and hugged us. We didn't let them off easy, either. We're talking good solid body-pressing hugs of several seconds. No one rejected the hugs, though. As confused as they were, everyone was in for a warm embrace.

Cwiz said to one particularly sweaty obese dude, "C'mon now, bring it in, big guy. Let's do this."

The man obliged and they made it happen, one long therapeutic hug that thousands of people had to just stand and watch. And those people knew they were next.

The hugging party caused the traffic—which was already horrible after the show under normal circumstances—to come to a standstill. This caused security to wonder what was going on.

You can imagine the radio traffic:

"Hey, what's going on over there?"

"We have several guys here that are stopping the guests to hug them."

"What?"

"Yeah, we have some unauthorized huggers here."

"Well, get them the hell out of there."

Three security guards in yellow jackets rushed over to us. I'll never forget what they said.

"Hey guys, listen, you need to stop hugging our guests."

"Or what?"

"Or we're kicking you out."

"For giving out hugs?"

"You heard me."

"Roger that. We're all hugged out anyway."

LIFE LESSON:
You need twelve hugs a day to grow, so start hugging it out.

CHAPTER **19**

Skinny-Dipping in the Dancing Waters

Before we had annual passes to get into Disneyland proper, we hung around Disneyland Hotel a lot, seeing what kind of trouble we could get into. We had apparently run out of targets in our part of Orange County, and we fanned out to Anaheim.

One day as we were wandering around the grounds looking for something to do, we saw a lot of people going into a convention hall. We were around twenty years old at the time. We were wearing shorts, T-shirts, and Teva sandals. The people milling about the convention were clearly all part of a company event, because many of them were wearing the same polo shirts and had lanyards with nametags dangling from their necks.

We wandered in with them to see what was going on, and immediately smelled food.

Cwiz looked at me and said, "You hungry?"

I said, "Starving."

Cwiz smiled. "Then let's eat."

We walked in like we owned the place, strolling through the registration and foyer area right into the main banquet hall. There were at least fifty circular tables, each with eight seats and a tablecloth, silverware, and centerpiece with flowers. The place was packed with employees engaged in loud conversation, and soft mellow music played from a stage where a PowerPoint presentation appeared to be paused.

We found a nearly empty table near the back and sat down. We tried our best to act like we belonged, but our T-shirts and dirty feet screamed otherwise. There were two guys already seated at our table who gave us sideways glances and then looked at each other, confused.

I said, "How are you guys doing?"

The older guy, with salt-and-pepper hair, a red polo shirt, and slacks, said, "I'm good, how are you guys?" He said it sarcastically, like he knew we did not belong.

Cwiz answered, "We're just trying to get through this thing, right? I'd rather be golfing."

The younger guy agreed. "No kidding. They need to hurry up." The younger guy clearly was not suspicious.

The PowerPoint screen changed and now said "Sav-On Drug Stores." I poked Cwiz stealthily and pointed to the screen.

The older guy asked, "What store are you guys with?"

Cwiz said, "Store 254."

"Which one?"

"254."

"Where's that?"

"Fountain Valley, right off the 405."

"Oh, okay, we're with one in LA."

"Yeah, Jim Kramer is our manager, but he couldn't make it, so he sent us down to see what's going on and report back."

"That's good. What's your guys' position there?"

Just then a waiter showed up and set down a lobster plate in front of each of us, saving us from answering the question, and we pretended we didn't hear it.

I said, "No, excuse me. I ordered the steak."

The waiter bowed slightly. "Very sorry, sir. I'll be right back."

I smiled at Cwiz and quietly whispered to him, "Damn right."

Cwiz cracked up, and we enjoyed our lunch.

This successful venture into the world of conventions and free lunches had us coming back again and again to the Disneyland Hotel. We would frequently go mid-week, in the middle of the afternoon when we were bored, and see what sort of food was being served. Cwiz got more and more brazen as the place started to feel more and more like home.

Sometimes we would go on weekends with large groups of friends. One time, we found ourselves there on a Friday night during a show called *The Dancing Waters,* which was a water show at the hotel where they pumped the water into the air in rhythmic patterns to the beat of music. Think of the Bellagio dancing waters show in Las Vegas, but at one-tenth the scale. As we watched the waters dance, Cwiz suddenly decided it would be fun to leap into the *Dancing Waters* pool.

The pool had lights and pumps and all sorts of electrical gadgets shooting the water up into the air. Hundreds of people were scattered around the pools, on bridges, and on the sides watching the water.

Cwiz found a quiet corner toward the back of the pool and disrobed. He jumped into the pool with his boxers on and started swimming toward the center, where the show was going on, and where the tourist cameras were pointed. When he got there, he took a deep breath, went underwater, pulled off his boxers, and let his naked butt ascend to the surface. Then he started dolphin-kicking across the pool, naked. I am still amazed he avoided getting arrested that night.

LIFE LESSON:
Act like you own the place.

Chapter 20

How Lovely Are Thy Branches

We always liked the energy of the Christmas season. There seemed to be more to do, more pranks to play, and more fun to have. One season, Cwiz, the Captain, and I decided to go caroling. You already know Cwiz isn't much of a singer. The Captain and I aren't exactly Frank Sinatras either. But for whatever reason, we thought it would be funny.

We went to South Coast Plaza (a mall here in OC that, I am told, rakes in more cash than just about any mall in the world) and perched ourselves in the busiest spot in the mall, at the busiest time of year. We were on the second floor, looking over an indoor plaza of sorts, where kids and their parents lined up to go on the carousel. We did not even take the time to dress up. We were wearing what we always wore back then: shorts, T-shirts, and Teva sandals.

We started our song in a strong baritone and projected as best we could.

"*Away in a manger/No crib for a bed....*"

Our voices rang off the walls and echoed powerfully. Then the mall broke. Shoppers stopped dead in their tracks. The carousel operator stared. The kids stopped sucking their lollipops. The stores seemed to stop operating. Everyone came out of whatever nook they were in to see what was going on. But nothing was going on, except that three bored idiots wanted to see what would happen if they just started singing Christmas carols. We followed that one up with "Rudolph" and then closed with "We Wish You a Merry Christmas." When we bowed, a few people clapped. Then we went to get some See's Candies samples.

A few days later, we were looking for something else to do,

when we realized that Christmas trees last only so long. When the holiday is over, the branches dry out and then every person on the block wakes up to realize that they are prominently displaying a fire hazard in their living room. On trash day the week after Christmas, the husks of former Christmas glory find themselves curbside with the torn packaging and uneaten fruitcakes.

For most people, these trees rotting next to the trash are hardly noticed. For us, though, it was an opportunity to play a pointless prank. On the night before trash day, wearing all black, we took Cwiz's truck and drove around our neighborhood looking for discarded trees.

We hit the mother lode. We collected the trees one by one and threw them in the back of the truck. Before long, the truck bed was completely filled up, with several dozen trees stacked high and strapped down.

We found a residential street with a greenbelt park on either side. We parked the truck and started unloading. We stacked the trees so that there was no way for traffic to get through.

Then, we drove around to a cul de sac nearby, parked, slinked into the greenbelt next to the trees, and waited for someone to drive into our trap. We lay in the wet grass with a clear view of the roadblock, just twenty-five feet in front of us, but we were invisible in the darkness. Before long, a sedan pulled up and then stopped ten feet from the trees. The car sat there without a movement for a long ten seconds, then quietly backed up and drove the other way.

We howled with laughter. I fully admit we were complete morons, like a toddler who learns that if he drops a cup of water, Mom or Dad has to clean it up, and then does it again and again. It was as if we were marveling that our stupid prank actually had an impact on another person. There was not much more to the prank than that. We could not even see the person's reactions, just the blank mechanical gleam of the car's headlights and then its painfully slow U-turn. Nevertheless, it was hilarious to us.

Another car pulled up, paused, and did the same thing. Then another. We continued to giggle away, lying in the dewy grass.

Then a truck pulled up, and this vehicle's driver appeared to be the sort of person who thought outside the box. After inspecting the situation, he pulled up and over the curb and went around the trees. This was beginning to look like an experiment in personality types.

Then another car pulled up, and this time, a man got out to inspect the trees. He left his door ajar and walked over to the trees. He walked up and down the line of trees four deep, and then he let out an exasperated, "What the hell is this?"

Being only a short distance away, we heard it perfectly over the idling engine, and this was too much for us. We cackled out loud and then quickly shushed ourselves. The dude heard us, looked our direction, and said, "Hey!"

We jumped up and ran in the opposite direction through the field in the greenbelt.

O'er the fields we go
Laughing all the way

The problem was that this greenbelt had exercise equipment sporadically located next to a jogging trail. There were spots here and there for people to do pull-ups, sit-ups, and other various plyometric exercises.

We were not all that familiar with the exact placement of these steel-reinforced items and could barely see a thing as we ran. So Cwiz unfortunately ran full speed into a shin-high bar that was cemented into the ground. There was a loud twang, and Cwiz went down in a heap, wailing in pain.

The Captain and I stopped and looked back. The man was just standing by his car, not pursuing.

Cwiz thought he had broken both legs. We got him up, and he limped back to the truck. Cwiz gimped around for several weeks after that. But if you asked him about it, he'd say it was completely worth it.

LIFE LESSON:
Celebrate the holidays like you mean it.

CHAPTER 21

THE JUICE

One late evening, while sipping Cokes at an all-night diner called Carrow's, Cwiz, the Captain, and I were commiserating with one another over the Captain's impending move to Northern California. The Captain had just graduated from college and had taken a job as a pastor at a church in Danville. It was the end of an era.

As we looked at each other and played with our straws, we knew our days of endlessly screwing around with one another were over. Cwiz started talking about how we needed to do something—something crazy, something big. He was fixated on the idea that we needed to put a cherry on top of our exploits. Cwiz was always talking about the passage of time, about memories, about making sure we didn't miss a second of it.

We knew Cwiz was right. We needed to do something epic to send off the Captain. We started brainstorming all kinds of stupid things we could do. Come up with a killer prank? Go somewhere we hadn't been? Pull off some weird stunt?

It came down to what was dominating everyone's attention. It was 1995. To be specific, the fall of 1995. There was one thing taking over everyone's water cooler conversation at that time: the OJ Trial.

For you younger folk, "OJ" refers to Orenthal James Simpson, an incredible college athlete turned professional football player turned commercial spokesperson turned movie star. Although OJ enjoyed a basically spotless reputation with the general public, he had suddenly killed two people (allegedly—ahem!) with a knife, taken off in his car with a friend, and led the police on a chase down the 405 freeway. He eventually turned himself in and the long, slow march to trial began. Everyone was glued to the OJ spectacle, and the trial was, before it started, already dubbed the "Trial of the Century" because of the sheer amount of network coverage and non-stop attention of the public.

The trial was already in full swing. Each morning, OJ's lawyers, some of whom were the most famous lawyers in the world and were now becoming celebrities in their own right, arrived at the courthouse with fanfare. Even the judge and the prosecutors were becoming household names. The scrutiny was intense, and every move was second-guessed and analyzed by the talking heads every night on CNN (and every other news channel).

Because the arrival of the lawyers every morning was a spectacle in itself, news trucks from all over the world, reporters with microphones, sound guys with boom microphones, courtroom staff, interested parties, and crazy people with signs all piled up behind caution tape erected by courthouse sheriffs. It was an absolute circus at the courthouse every day, and we had seen it daily on TV. What better place for a couple of clowns?

Our brilliant idea was to go down to the courthouse and join the mêlée the following morning—meaning, in four hours. It was about 2 a.m. when the idea surfaced at Carrow's Diner, and we would need to head up to LA by 6 a.m. to get there for the 8:30 a.m. start when the lawyers arrived. The question was what to do when we got there.

What we ultimately decided to do makes no sense at all. It takes some background explanation to even begin to understand. You see, the Captain liked to do this weird thing. He liked to impersonate a lizard. More accurately, he liked to do an impression of a violently berserk Lizard Man on PCP.

It all started at a church camp for teenagers. During some kind of talent show, the Captain would come flailing out of the bushes at the kids, wearing nothing but board shorts. He would hiss, crawl on his belly, and flip himself end over end in the dirt. Covered now in filth, he would stand up, but while hunched over, he would emit a piercing, horrifying, high-pitched shriek. The sound of the shriek would shock the kids and send them into hysterics.

It was truly astounding that this grown man could make such a noise come out of his face. The Captain would then crawl around some more in the dirt, maybe lick somebody's foot or other body part, and then slither back into the bushes. As you might imagine, this would freak the crap out of the kids, but in a good way. Ian called this impersonation the Lizard Man. As I said, it doesn't make a lot of sense, but it was objectively ridiculous and hilarious, and that was really all that mattered.

So, at Carrow's that night, the thought came to us: "What if Lizard Man showed up at the OJ trial?"

And the Captain said, "You mean the Lizard of Justice," with a knowing, maniacal grin.

This was our grand idea. The three of us crumpled in laughter in the booth, and we knew exactly what we were doing in the morning. We all went home for three or four hours of sleep and agreed to meet at Cwiz's house for the drive up to the courthouse in LA at 6:30.

I rolled up the next morning with a video camera and my regular camera with actual rolls of 35mm film. The Captain brought nothing but balloons, as in the balloons with which you make balloon animals. On the drive up, we did not discuss much of a plan. The plan was merely to arrive, check out the circus, and have the Lizard of Justice show up and do his thing.

We found a place to park and walked a few blocks to the Criminal Courts Building. We could hear someone yelling a block away that hell awaited those who did not repent. When we got closer, we saw the yeller was wearing a straw hat to protect him from the sun's rays. He also had a bullhorn and hand-painted signs. Apparently, he was planning to spend the day there converting the world's reporters who were assigned to the front of the courthouse. We ducked under the decibels coming from the bullhorn and pushed our way into the crowd.

On either side of the entrance to the courthouse, crowds waited for the celebrity lawyers to arrive. A lane 6 feet wide ran down the middle of the crowd to permit people with legitimate business at the court to enter. Security tape separated the two sides. Officers with guns on their hips patrolled the crowds, looking annoyed. There were probably 250 people there simply to watch the spectacle unfold.

We gathered and developed a plan that was brilliant in its simplicity. The plan was this: when famous lawyer Robert Shapiro arrived and stepped out of his car, the Lizard of Justice would appear. Cwiz and I would prime the crowd for the Lizard Man's appearance and record the event for posterity.

As the Captain quietly found a place in the crowd of reporters next to a block wall on one side of the security tape, Cwiz and I started milling around the crowd on the other side of the tape. Our plan was to photograph and videotape the Lizard Man's appearance from across the lane when Shapiro showed up. We pulled out balloons and started making balloon animals for the people in the crowd. We made balloon flowers, dogs, bears, kitties, pregnant dogs, funny hats, and swords. People asked us what we were doing there, and we said that we had heard that the Lizard of Justice was coming down here today and we wanted to see for ourselves.

They'd ask, "Who is the Lizard of Justice?"

"You haven't heard of him?!"

"No."

"He's a crime fighter of sorts. But perhaps more urban folklore than reality. He's like Spiderman or something, but he's the Lizard Man, er, of Justice. He has strong views on this case, apparently."

"Are you serious?"

"Dead serious. We heard the Lizard of Justice is coming today, like right now."

"What does he look like?"

"We don't know, but we've heard him scream before."

"Huh?"

Just then, a roar broke out from the crowd of reporters. Johnny Cochrane, OJ's lead trial lawyer, had arrived. The reporters all yelled out their questions to him simultaneously, and he hustled down the cordoned-off walkway, each reporter individually struggling to be heard above the others. "Johnny! Johnny! Why play the race card?!" He did not stop, did not answer any questions, and quickly walked into the courthouse.

Cwiz and I looked at each other and then shot a "thumbs up" to the Captain, who was mingling with the reporters on the other side. When Barry Scheck, OJ's defense lawyer with expertise in DNA analysis, showed up and also hustled by quickly, we knew Shapiro would be here any minute.

And then Shapiro arrived. The reporters again started screaming their questions. I saw the Captain suddenly disappear from view as he dropped down to the ground to disrobe. He pulled off his hoodie and his shoes and was now only in his shorts. His face emerged from the crowd of reporters, but he was no longer the Captain. He was the Lizard of Justice. His face morphed into a determined scowl.

In a flash, the Lizard of Justice leapt onto the brick wall above the reporters. He knelt on the wall, put his ten individual fingers next to his feet, which were balancing on the wall, took a deep breath, lifted his head, and discharged a long, inhuman screech. As he did so, his eyes looked toward the clouds, and his veins pulsed from his neck.

Every camera, every reporter, and every gun-toting cop turned toward him. The cops' dominant hands instinctively dropped to their weapons. Cameras flashed. A hush fell over the crowd. For his part, Shapiro got the hell out of Dodge. Not knowing what the Lizard of Justice might do, he hightailed it out of there through the courthouse's front door.

The full attention of every reporter, cop, and bystander was on the Lizard of Justice. An unnerving quiet suddenly descended on the crowd. *What will he say? What is he doing? Is he a good Lizard Man or a bad Lizard Man?*

You could feel the crowd lean in to hear what he would say.

Just then, the Lizard of Justice shrieked at the top of his lungs, so loud that his voice cracked, "*I AM THE LIZARD OF JUSTICE!*" And then he unleashed a second, long screech, a Jurassic scream not heard on Earth for epochs. The reporters around him backed up, and a circle of space opened around him in the crowd.

Cwiz and I were in hysterics, but I tried to stay still for the shot. A particularly large specimen of a police officer ran over, and yelled at the Lizard of Justice, "What the hell are you doing? Get down from there right now!"

The Lizard of Justice quickly complied, hopped down into the crowd of reporters, and disappeared in the mass of confusion. He reappeared as the Captain, wearing his hoodie and looking around sheepishly. The cops looked confused and the reporters were perplexed, but as he walked away toward Cwiz and me, the courthouse routine simply resumed. The circus went on without us.

To this day, in my law office, I have a picture of the Lizard of Justice screeching on top of the courthouse wall. Robert Shapiro is in the foreground, and a fat dude stands there holding a balloon and enjoying himself. To me, it's one of the best photographs ever taken.

LIFE LESSON:
Make sure to celebrate the end of an era, because nothing lasts forever.

The Lizard of Justice picture that resides in my office.

CHAPTER 22

You Guys a Couple of Clowns?

We were driving down a twisting two-lane road at a steep incline. A cooler in the truck's flatbed strained against a bungee cord as we made seemingly never-ending sharp turns into Yosemite Valley. Every few minutes, skyscraping redwoods would part and reveal a precipitous abyss. If we ran off this road, it was 5,000 feet straight down to the valley floor.

The view from Glacier Point, where we were traveling from, is arguably one of the best views in the world. Half Dome looms on one side, with El Capitan on the other and a gloriously deep and rich river valley in the middle. While we were at that point a half hour before, Cwiz and I had tried to see who could take the more ridiculously dangerous photograph. We first took the usual photographs standing at the guard rail and smiling. But those left us unsatisfied. We wanted a picture that, when you looked at it later, would make your hands sweat.

So, one at a time, we climbed over the safety rail and carefully walked to the edge of the cliff. There was one spot where a slim finger of rock jutted out over the abyss, ending with a small pedestal on the end of the rock's finger. The pedestal was perhaps ten inches wide and hung in mid-air over thousands of feet of freefall. We debated whether we should risk the shot on the little pedestal. But Cwiz was game, as I knew he would be. He was always willing to gamble big, hoping for a big payoff. It was his nature.

Cwiz went first. He scooted out on the pedestal, got his feet under him, and stood up slowly with his knees visibly shaking. His toes hung over the pedestal, and his knees were touching as he tried to straighten his spine and smile. I got the shot and told him to hurry back to the other side of the rail before he killed himself. Then it was my turn. I did the same thing as he took the picture and I tried not to whizz my shorts.

Feeling like we had defied death, we hopped into Cwiz's truck, giddy at how cool the pictures would look. But in his truck, flying down the side of the mountain to the valley, it occurred to me that Cwiz's driving was far more dangerous than our photo shoot. He stomped on the gas and passed the slow drivers in front of us around one blind corner after another. An accident on that road, and at that speed, undoubtedly would have sent us over the side, and it would have been a full minute before we hit the ground, instantly disintegrating us.

Nevertheless, we made it to the valley, managing to stay alive but royally pissing off every single driver we encountered. We were not long in the valley when we heard the short burst of a police vehicle announcing its presence ("*Blooooop*") and saw the flashing lights in the mirrors. Cwiz pulled over into a shallow ditch, crunching gravel and laying the weeds down with his tires.

The cop took his time coming to the truck. We looked at each other nervously. It was peaceful and beautiful on the valley floor.

"You are an idiot," I said.

"Be cool."

Cwiz rolled his window down, put his hands at 10 and 2, and we waited.

The cop moseyed over, took a long look at the open bed of the truck, and said, "You boys know why I pulled you over?"

"No, sir," said Cwiz.

"We got some calls that a green Ford F150 truck with two guys in it was driving recklessly down the hill from Glacier Point. That you guys?"

"I don't know," said Cwiz.

"Sure seems like it's you guys, doesn't it?"

The cop leered at us through his sunglasses and leaned in for a long look.

I looked straight ahead.

Cwiz said, "I don't know, sir."

"You guys comin' from Glacier Point?"

"Yes, sir."

"And where you headed?"

"We're leaving. We're on our way to visit a friend up north and we just stopped by to see the view."

"I see." The cop looked around the cab suspiciously and said, "Have you guys been drinkin'?"

"No, sir."

The cop jerked his chin toward the truck bed and said, "What's in the cooler?"

"Nothing."

"You're saying it's empty?"

"No, it's not empty, but we haven't been drinking."

"So what's in it?"

"Balloons."

"Balloons?"

"Yes, sir."

"And what are you doin' with balloons in a cooler?"

"We make balloon animals."

"Like a clown? You guys a couple of clowns?"

"No, we're not clowns, sir. We make balloon animals, and you have to keep the balloons cool, or they won't work properly. So we carry the cooler around to keep the balloons cool."

"What are the balloons for?"

Cwiz smiled and said, "Well, the ladies like 'em."

The cop offered a half grin in return. "Then you won't mind if I take a look, right?"

"No, sir. Be my guest."

The cop walked back, reached into the bed, and grabbed the cooler. He opened it up and found three bags of uninflated, multi-colored, perfectly chilly balloons for making balloon animals.

He walked back to the cab. "Well, that's a first. Drive safely, boys. Listen, if I get another call about a green F150, things will be different. Understood?"

"Yes, sir."

LIFE LESSON:

Learn the majestic art of ballooning, because it comes in handy more often than you would think.

CHAPTER 23

JERRY-RIGGING

As I mentioned earlier, Cwiz and I were security guards at Fountain Valley High School for a couple years. But the term "security guards" is a little strong for what we actually were, which was basically teenagers with walkie-talkies. They gave us a walkie-talkie and a hat that said "Security" on it. That was it. With no courses, manuals, or kung fu training, we were officially put in charge of securing the safety of 2,000 students on campus. We started patrolling the grounds together, which was absurd on so many levels.

In the first place, we had recently graduated from this same school, so we still knew many of the kids who had been either sophomores or freshmen while we were attending the school. These kids were not going to listen to us.

Second, we were two single nineteen-year-old dudes far more interested in ogling the eighteen-year-old girls walking around the campus than making sure they got to class on time. One of the other security guys told me that FVHS was one of the few schools in the district that had not had a security guard impregnate one of their students. They attributed FVHS's remarkable success in this regard to hiring guys from the local church, on the theory that religious dudes would not be as horny, which is just precious.

Anyway, Cwiz and I were tasked with walking around campus, looking for taggers, making sure kids got to class after the bell rang, ensuring that no unauthorized people came on campus, pulling kids out of class and bringing them to the principal's office for one reason or another, and occasionally breaking up fights.

But 95 percent of the time, nothing happened. We worked from noon to 4 p.m., which meant that for half our shift, there were hardly any students on campus, because most of the students were done with school at 2:10 p.m.

Cwiz and I were supposed to spread out and cover different areas of the school, so he was usually at one end of the school and I was at the other, to ensure we had eyes on the critical entry points.

We loafed around the campus, joked around and flirted with the students between bells, and after the students were tucked away in their classes, we had nothing to do but wander around and communicate with one another on the walkie-talkies.

For some reason, the school administrators spoke in formal police jargon on the radios, using police codes. All of the principals, a few of the head secretaries, and security personnel had radios. Approximately ten to twelve people at the school had them, and anything that was said could be heard by all people with a radio.

If the principal, who was designated as No. 1, wanted to speak with the vice principal, Mr. Christensen (No. 2), you would hear him say:

"No. 1 to No. 2."

Christensen (No. 2) would respond, "Go ahead."

No. 1 would say: "10-20?" (Which means "What is your location?")

"Cafeteria."

"10-4." (Which means 10-4.)

When Cwiz and I communicated, we would follow suit, but since we were not important enough to be given designated numerical code names, we started using our normal nicknames.

Our conversations would typically go like this:

"Cwiz to Herm." (Cwiz had nicknamed me Herm.)

"Go ahead."

"10-20?"

"Pool deck."

"10-4."

These "10" codes would be used all day, all the time, for everything. Cwiz and I thought it was funny that chubby administrators enjoyed talking to each other like cops through Radio Shack walkie-talkies. So, as time went on, we grew more and more bold with our radio communications with one another. Our radio calls became more and more silly as we made fun of the administrators, especially in the 3 p.m. to 4 p.m. hour, when most of the bosses were already gone. In those hours, our accents, pronunciations, and stated situations became outrageously stupid.

"Herm to Cwiz."

"Go heh."

"Yeahhhhhaahhhhhh, we got a situation here. We got a truck jack-knifed in the tennis court."

"Roger that. Any injuries?"

"One cat and two llamas."

"10-4, ambulance en route."

We cracked ourselves up daily over the radio, trying to outdo each other with outrageous fake calamities befalling the school.

"Cwiz to Herm."

"Go heh."

"I need immediate backup."

"Describe the problem, if you please."

"There's a walrus flatlining on the pool deck. Bring the shock paddles."

"10-4. On the way."

Some of the other radio carriers did not think our use of the radio was appropriate; we had a few detractors. One of them was a janitor named Jerry. Jerry was one of these oafy maintenance types who was perpetually unable to get his belt to do its job. His blue janitor pants were always sagging down under the strain of his adequate belly, and the quarter slot was always open.

I am sorry to say Jerry was a sort of pathetic creature, apparently cursed by God, always banging his head on an air conditioning unit, falling off a ladder, or otherwise whining about some difficulty in his work. As such, and because he was one of our detractors, he was endlessly entertaining to us as the butt of our jokes.

Over time, whenever Cwiz had to communicate with Jerry, he would pronounce his name in a deliberately strange way to see if Jerry ever noticed. This little habit of Cwiz's may have had something to do with Jerry not liking us, but he never acknowledged the pronunciation problems to us. Cwiz and Jerry would have to communicate over the radio from time to time, and Cwiz always used the opportunity to tease him.

"Jerry to Caesar."

"Caesar here. How can I help you, Yerry."

"I've seen some kids over here behind Room 214."

"10-4 Jhurrrry, I'll head right over."

"Roger, thanks, over and out."

Over time, the pronunciation of "Jerry" transformed from Choory, to Jury, to Yury, to Zhjhurrrrry, which sounded like Chewbacca was saying it. Cwiz's goal, as always, was to see if he could crack me up in front of Jerry, which would make it obvious we were making fun of him.

After a while, Cwiz would address "Yuuuurry" right to his face in such an aggressive, loud, and drawn-out manner that it appeared Cwiz was suffering from a mini-stroke as he said the name. I would have to turn around and leave before I busted up.

To this day, when we meet a Jerry, we look at each other and laugh like juvenile hyenas from the memory of these encounters.

LIFE LESSON:
If you can make work fun, you should.

Chapter 24

FOR THE FREE CREAM

At the same time we were working at FVHS, Cwiz was also volunteering as a college leader at church. From time to time, the college group tried to raise money for camps. They would ask Cwiz to try to get stores to offer free products and services for the fundraisers.

At that time, four high school kids from the church worked at the Baskin-Robbins 31 Flavors ice cream store nearby. So Cwiz walked in one day to see if he could get the manager to offer some free stuff for the fundraiser and to say hi to the students he knew. One of the high school students, Sam, jokingly offered Cwiz an employment application.

Sam said, "Want to work here?"

Cwiz responded, "Why not?"

Cwiz started filling out the application.

Name?

"Cwiz Ruiz."

Address?

"1234 Chimichurri Street."

Employment History?

"Clown."

He filled out the rest of the application in this ridiculous fashion but left his real phone number. To his surprise, the owner called him the next day and asked him if he wanted a job.

"Why not?"

When he showed up on the first day of work, the owner explained to him that she employed a lot of high school kids. She said that she needed someone to set a good example for them, someone more responsible to keep the others in line.

"Look no further," he said.

Cwiz was already working at least three other jobs, as a security guard, a sometimes valet, and, on the weekends, a balloon artist. He did not have a lot of time to scoop ice cream, but he carved out a few hours every couple days. The obvious draw was the free ice cream.

On his first day, Sam gave him a polo shirt and a brown visor to wear. Then he showed Cwiz how the owner wanted them to weigh every single scoop on a tiny scale, to make sure that no customer received more than the correct number of ounces of ice cream.

"You weigh every scoop, every time," Sam said. "Those are the rules."

"Are you serious?" asked Cwiz.

"Yeah, she will catch you if you don't weigh."

"How?"

"She watches us."

"How?"

"She sits across the parking lot and looks through the windows at us with binoculars." Sam pointed through the large pane glass window across a wide parking lot.

Cwiz said, "No way!" He started cracking up. He had already formulated a plan.

On his second day, perhaps four hours of total time at the new job, he was bored. A family pulled up and started making their way into the store. As soon as the door opened, Cwiz started yelling and banging on a pot with a spoon. The other customers in the store spun around to see what was amiss.

Cwiz yelled out, "Congratulations! You're our 100th customer today! Hurray!"

Cwiz's co-worker that day, Nina, looked scared, not knowing what was going on. The family's eyes widened, and they looked around.

Cwiz yelled again, "You did it! Congratulations! Anything you want is on the house!" But then he dropped his voice, "Except for the cakes—not those. But anything else. Want a banana split?"

On the third shift he worked, he organized a game of hot lava with the employees. A young couple walked in the store to find Cwiz and two other employees standing on the counters, trying to leap from one to the other.

When Cwiz saw them, he yelled out, "Congratulations! You're the 100,000th customer! Ice cream on the houuuuuuuussseee!"

On the fourth shift he worked, he saw the owner parked in her car far across the parking lot, just as Sam had warned. Cwiz could see her binoculars trained on the store windows. There were no congratulations to the customers that day. That is, until she pulled away.

The next day Cwiz brought his own binoculars from home. Eventually, the manager pulled up to start spying. She pulled out her binoculars, adjusted the width of the lenses, trained them on the store window, altered the focus until it was just so, and found herself looking directly at Cwiz, who was looking back at her with his own binoculars. He could barely keep the focus on her, as he was giggling uncontrollably.

Cwiz, who never wanted the job in the first place, quit before she could fire him.

LIFE LESSON:
Life is short. Eat more ice cream.

Chapter 25

Selling Jeeps

Cwiz was at a department store looking for a button-up shirt. He needed business attire appropriate for a car salesman. It was his first day of work at the Jeep dealership in Huntington Beach. He found an inoffensive gray starched shirt with white buttons for less than $20. He put on some black slacks, a black belt, black socks, and black shoes. Without time to even wash or iron the new shirt, he showed up to work for his first afternoon shift. The crinkled lines of the shirt, which had been folded in a square to fit into the plastic packaging, were still clearly visible.

When he arrived at the dealership, he was informed that a monthly sales meeting was scheduled. Twenty or so salesmen, all in worn suits and ties, sat around drinking stale coffee in a room lit by fluorescence. The sales manager, a man named Kazz who had a thick accent, announced that Trevor had won the salesman of the month. He held up a check for $5,000 and showed it to the envious crowd, who reluctantly clapped as Trevor proudly walked to the front to accept his check.

Kazz introduced Cwiz to the group, asking them to welcome their newest salesman. Kazz added that he was also the youngest and asked the guys to look out for him and show him the ropes.

Trevor said, "Sure thing, Kazz. I'll take him to buy a real suit."

The group laughed.

Nodding his head as though in resignation, Cwiz saw in his mind's eye his future self, taking that bonus check from Kazz's hand the following month and wiping the grin off Trevor's face. Right after the group meeting, Cwiz sat down behind Kazz's desk for a private meeting.

Kazz said, "Listen, Caesar, I'm going to put you on Trevor's team."

Cwiz said, "You're the boss."

"That means you'll be competing with him, but don't let it get you down. You'll learn from him, and in time, you could be doing really well here. You're young, and it's going to take some time."

"Don't worry about me."

Kazz said, "You know, I normally don't hire guys like you. I hire family men. Guys who have mouths to feed at home, you understand me? I like guys who are hungry."

"I'm gonna be fine. In fact, my prediction is that you'll be giving that bonus check to me next month."

Kazz laughed. "Well, you better get to work then. But keep in mind, there's a pecking order here. You have to put your name on the board and take your turn with the customers that come in."

Cwiz left the office, put his name on the board, and waited his turn to meet his first customer. For an hour, he strolled the parking lot, checking out the features on the new Jeeps, while Hootie and the Blowfish played on the parking lot speakers.

His first customer turned out to be a young guy with a new job who was looking to get some new wheels. He brought his girlfriend with him, and they wanted a Jeep Wrangler. The customer was eager, and Cwiz was excited to sell it to him. They lightly haggled over the price of the car, settling on a number, and Cwiz immediately went into Kazz's office to find out what he would make.

Cwiz said, "So, we settled on $13,250."

Kazz said, "Okay, great."

"What'll I make on the sale?"

"$100."

"$100?!"

Kazz looked tired. "Look, there's no profit in a Wrangler. It's the cheapest car on the lot. If you want to make some money, sell him some accessories. You get 25 percent on any accessories you sell."

Cwiz walked back to his customers.

"So, listen, we're good. What do you want to do about the rims?"

"What do you mean?"

"The rims on the car are the basics. You should think about upgrading those babies."

"I don't know, man. They're fine."

The customer's girlfriend looked annoyed, and she got up and went to the bathroom.

Cwiz leaned in. "Look, man. We're talking about rims here. What about the ladies?"

But when Cwiz said "ladies," he drew out the word, saying "laaaaaaadies."

The customer smiled and looked behind him toward the bathroom. "Damn, I didn't even think about the laaaadies!" He elongated the word in the same way Cwiz did.

"Exactly." Cwiz nodded.

"Alright, man, slap those bad boys on!"

The rims were $2,000, so Cwiz went from making $100 to $600 on his first sale.

At the end of the first day, Cwiz picked Kazz's brain about the exact nature of sales and commissions. He was looking for an angle. Kazz explained to him that the real money was in bonuses. There were weekend bonuses of $1,000 for the salesman that sold the most cars. There were monthly bonuses of up to $5,000, like the one Trevor got. So, if he could sell the most cars, he would get the bonuses.

Cwiz quickly realized he did not need to gouge every customer to try to get them to pay way over invoice. If he could sell the cars at invoice, every customer would get a great deal, and he would get his $100. But, more importantly, he would win the weekend and monthly bonuses.

Cwiz immediately implemented this strategy. When a customer would walk onto the lot, he would tell them openly that he wanted to get them the best deal possible, that he would even sell them the car at invoice, because he was trying to become the salesman of the month to get a bonus. It was a win-win, he explained to them. He let the customer in on his secret, and because the customer was getting a good deal and he was not trying to nickel and dime them (except for a few more sales of rims), the cars were flying off the lot.

Kazz obviously saw what Cwiz was doing, selling one car after another without hard bargaining. But Kazz was happy because the dealership was also receiving bonuses from Chrysler (the Jeep manufacturer), and the more cars sold, the better the dealership did as a whole. The dealership also benefitted by turning the car sales into repair relationships with their customers. Cwiz was working the angles while the average salesman was not paying attention to the back-end details of manufacturer incentives.

For the months of January through May, Trevor had been the salesman of the month. But at the end of June—his first month at the dealership—it was Cwiz who stood up in front of all the salesmen to accept his monthly bonus check, with a wink to Trevor on the way up.

Life Lesson:

Before you can win the game, you have to understand the rules.

CHAPTER 26

NEGATIVE MACHISMO

Cwiz's boss, Kazz, was leaving the Jeep dealership and heading to Ford. He asked Cwiz, his number-one salesman, to go with him, and Cwiz was happy to do so. But at Ford, he was starting over, and he could see right away that this dealership's culture was more confrontational. The sales team was full of alpha males, all intent on being the best. A sort of pent-up, negative machismo hung in the smoke-filled air of the back lot where the salesmen took their cigarette breaks.

Ford used what they called an "up" system in order to determine whose turn it was to approach a new customer. Names were chosen at random and then listed on a wipe-away board at the back of the dealership near the car wash station, like a batting order in baseball. The name at the top of the board was the leadoff hitter, and he got the first customer who showed up. The second name got the second customer, and so on throughout the day. The point of the "up" system was to ensure that every salesman got a fair shot at approximately the same number of customers per day.

One of Cwiz's fellow salesmen was a big dude from New York. He had the over-the-top stereotypical NYC accent, and he liked to play it up, like it transformed him into some sort of tough guy from a mobster movie. This guy—let's call him John—started jumping the batting order and stealing ups from his fellow salesmen.

The unfortunate victim would be standing around the board, near the car wash station, having a smoke break, and when a customer would walk in, even though John was several names down the list, he would walk off to engage the customer. The guy who was up would call out, "What the hell?" John would turn around, walking backwards with his palms to the sky, and claim it was a returning customer coming to see him.

Cwiz watched the other salesmen cower at the guy and do nothing while this guy stole the ups. It did not sit well with him. Cwiz asked the guy who had just been sniped, "Why'd you let him do that?"

"You're saying you'd do something about it?"

"Yeah, I would."

"I'm not worried about it. He sucks, so he needs the sales."

Cwiz said, "Well he's not stealing my up."

But it wasn't long before John did. As Cwiz was yukkin' it up with the guys, waiting for his customer to come in, he saw a truck pull up in the customer lot. As he started to approach, John suddenly appeared out of nowhere to chat with the customer. A few hours later, John made the sale, and Cwiz fumed, watching him close the deal.

After his successful sale, John was enjoying a smoke break with the guys in the back near the car wash, savoring every inhale. John straddled a small drain in the middle of the street that was doing its job, draining dirty water and suds from the wash.

Cwiz walked right up to him. "John, just so you know, you do that again to me, we're gonna have a problem."

John pulled his cigarette out of his mouth. "Do what exactly?"

"Steal my up."

Predictably, like he had seen in a mobster movie, John threw his cigarette straight down into the water and said, "What are you gonna do about it?"

He stepped forward and shoved Cwiz with a stiff arm to the shoulder. The four other salesmen standing there fanned out with widened eyes.

Then, without any hesitation, in one decisive move, Cwiz kicked John in the balls. Hard.

John immediately crumpled into the gutter in a fetal position, holding his nads. He had suds in his hair and his suit was soaked.

Cwiz stood over him. "Don't even think about doing it again." Then he walked away.

The four other salesmen were holding each other, hooting with laughter. Cwiz was now their leader. John went home that day to change his suit. He came back the next day and it was as if nothing had ever happened, except John stopped stealing ups, from anyone. They never spoke of it, and not even Kazz said a word about the incident to him.

LIFE LESSON:
If you find yourself in a fight, better to end it before it starts.

CHAPTER 27

BAPTIZING FLIPPER

Our church liked to baptize people, which makes sense, because it was a Baptist church. The baptizee, wearing a special white robe for the occasion, crosses their arms over their chest, the pastor puts one hand on their back, and one hand on their crossed hands in front, and dunks them. The penitent goes completely under and comes up clean as a whistle, usually snorting water from their nose, and ready to live their new life.

In order to watch this experience while you are sitting in church, you need a pool, or a large jacuzzi at least, actually installed in the sanctuary. So when a Baptist church is being constructed from the ground up, you have to hire a pool contractor, because Baptists are into full immersion. None of this measly sprinkling about the head. They go full dunk tank.

Our church's dunk tank (or jacuzzi) was in the back of the center of the church stage in the main sanctuary. The pool could not be seen from the seats. It was there, but it was concealed behind the back wall. When someone was being baptized, you could see them only from about mid-waist up, as they stood in the elevated jacuzzi at the back of the stage.

On baptism days, which were usually once a month for new members, there was a special time in the service when the pastor would suddenly appear in a robe behind the back wall. A microphone from the ceiling picked up the sound of the water sloshing around in the unseen pool as the pastor moved around. After a few words, the baptizee would wade into the pool and the dunking would occur.

But on non-baptism days, the jacuzzi would be drained and you could get inside. If you did, you could poke your head up and look at the congregation while they looked directly at you behind the pastor's lectern.

One day, during a Sunday morning service on a non-baptism day, the congregation sat and listened attentively to our pastor as he delivered opening remarks and announcements.

I turned to the Captain. "Where's Cwizzy?"

He shrugged. "He was here a second ago."

When we turned to look around, we heard some snickering from the front rows where the high school students sat. When I looked up to see what was going on, I saw a pointy blue thing sticking up from behind our pastor. Something was in the baptismal.

A snout of some kind slowly and sneakily poked up behind the pastor as he talked. The pastor continued with his announcements, unaware of what was going on.

The snout rose higher, and then an entire dolphin head could be seen.

Cwiz had, for some reason, found a rubber dolphin mask that you could wear on top of your head. The rubber dolphin head covered his hair, leaving his face visible, and the bottlenose stuck straight up on top, like a conehead.

While kneeling down in the jacuzzi, Cwiz bobbed up and down, so the congregation could see only what appeared to be a dolphin playing around in the baptismal, perhaps hoping to be fed. An "eek, eek, eek" sound could be heard as Cwiz did his best impression of Flipper.

When the laughter grew too loud, the pastor turned around to see what was going on.

"Oh my, is that a dolphin?

More laughing.

The pastor said, "My money is on Caesar." And then he made some lame joke like, "What is the porpoise of that?" That drew a few scattered laughs, and some groans.

There was a purpose, though. Cwiz wanted to make his buddies laugh, and he succeeded. We were dying.

LIFE LESSON:
For God's sake, keep your faith fun.

CHAPTER 28

I Pity the Fool

I showed up to Cwiz's house one day to find a beat-up 1980s GMC van in the driveway. It was a faded orange color.

"What is this doing here?"

Cwiz looked mischievous. "That's my new van."

"Why?"

Cwiz said nothing, but he gestured for me to come look in his garage. He walked toward the garage and pointed at a box containing numerous cans of black spray paint.

I said, "So, you're going to hire an army of six-year-olds to spray paint 'Cwiz Was Here' on every blank wall in the city?"

Cwiz smirked. "Better than that. We are going to transform this beauty," he pointed at the van, "into the A-Team van."

The A-Team was a television show that aired between 1983 and 1987. It was about a ragtag group of ex–Army officers, now soldiers of fortune, who lived in the shadows and helped people solve crimes without the help of the police. As the tagline of the show went, "If you have a problem…if no one else can help…and if you can find them…maybe you can hire the A-Team." Then the music would start, "Dah da da dah, da da dum," and the shiny black A-Team van would come barreling around a corner, cops giving chase, with the wheels screeching, and smoke and dust clouding behind. The four members of the A-Team, badasses one and all, would smile as they fled the scene of some epic and daring adventure.

Cwiz and I were ten years old when this show aired for the first time, and yeah, to us, it was a mind-blowing, life-altering show! I mean, Mr. T himself was driving the van! Because the show held a special place in my heart, I was beyond stoked about this van. First, the van was spray-painted flat black from stem to stern. Through the creative use of duct tape, a red stripe was painted down the side, just like the real thing from the TV show. Cwiz was later able to find a roof foil, which he duct-taped to the top of the van, again mimicking the real thing.

Over time, Cwiz added more and more accoutrements to the vehicle. All the seats in the back were removed and plush shag carpeting was added, wall to wall. I mean, literally, the floors and the walls were covered with carpeting. I can only imagine how the father of any girl who entered the van must have felt. Cwiz also added a public address system so that he could, like a cop, address people on the street as he was driving—which , you know, makes for a good time.

The van, once complete, cried out for a road trip. And thankfully, a music festival was coming up. It was 1996, and the first annual Tibetan Freedom concert was taking place in San Francisco, 450 miles to the north.

Cwiz invited a group of seven guys and gals who all agreed to drive up in the van for the festival. The group left at an ungodly hour, and six of them piled on top of each other in the back with no seats and no seatbelts. A guy named Scott was asleep in the passenger's bucket seat as Cwiz rocketed the A-Team van up north.

As Scott tells it, he was awakened from his sleep with the words, "Dude, take the wheel." The first thing he saw was an empty driver's seat as the van hurtled down the freeway. Cwiz had jumped up from the driver's seat, dived into the back of the van with the rest of the group, and started rolling around like an idiot. The van was doing about 75 mph at the time.

Everyone was screaming. Scott lunged for the wheel, and the van started to career to the left. Scott jumped into the driver's seat and overcompensated the sway as he panicked. The van headed toward the center divider of dirt. He finally gained control of the van, but only after it was in the center of the grassy median. The van came to a halt in a cloud of dust. Everyone was piled on top of each other and terrified. Then they all started laughing.

Scott says the most amazing thing about the whole episode is that Cwiz somehow convinced the entire group that it was Scott's fault they almost died. *Scott, you should not have jerked the wheel like that! You almost got us killed!* Ten years later, when Cwiz was hired as Scott's real estate agent in a home purchase, Scott asked Cwiz to pay recompense by giving him a discount on the sales commission. Cwiz agreed.

LIFE LESSON:
Never get into a windowless van.

CHAPTER 29

THE TERRORIST

Cwiz was arrested for felony terrorism. It was not as bad as it sounds, though. What happened was this: he created a bomb, and it blew up at somebody's house. Okay, that still sounds bad. I'll try this a different way and start from the beginning.

Cwiz and four other dudes were at his house, bored and looking for something to do. They knew that some of their girl pals were hanging out at their house just a few blocks away. This was the typical origin story for a prank. If there were two homes, one full of girls at a sleepover and another full of guys hanging out, then it was a near guarantee that one of the groups would attempt to play a prank on the other group.

One of the guys had heard that if you take dry ice and bottle it up, the gas will eventually expand in the bottle and the thing will blow up. This sounded like as good an idea as any, so they went out and somehow located some dry ice. They also bought two-liter Coke bottles, drank the Coke, and then filled the bottles up with dry ice.

Not knowing how long it would take for the gas to expand in the bottles, they drove immediately over to the house where all the girls were sleeping over, and threw the dry ice bombs into the bushes in the backyard.

There was one huge problem with the plan. The girls were staying at Erin's house, and Erin's dad was a lieutenant with the Santa Ana Police Department. This meant Cwiz and his co-conspirators had just thrown explosives onto a policeman's property, which is not usually a good idea.

A short while later, after the guys had driven back to Cwiz's house, the bottles exploded, ripping up the landscaping and scaring the bejesus out of the girls at the house. Car alarms erupted all over the block. Windows rattled for hundreds of yards around ground zero, and several frightened residents called the police.

The cops were there investigating the scene in no time. Soon enough, they figured out that this was a prank of some sort, and that the girls must know who the likely culprits were. And they did.

Cwiz picked up the phone at his house when it rang within fifteen minutes of the explosion. The boys were all hanging out, enjoying the success of their prank.

"Is this Caesar?" said a policeman.

"Yes."

"This is Officer Sobchek. I am at your friend Erin's house. We have quite a mess over here, as I am sure you can understand given what you dropped in the backyard."

"What?"

"You guys are not in trouble, but there is a mess over here that needs to be cleaned up."

"Okay."

"Do you understand me?"

"Yes, sir."

"Okay, then. I want you and all of the other guys that were responsible for making this mess to come over here right now and clean it up."

"Okay."

When Cwiz and the others arrived to clean up, they were promptly arrested, cuffed, and stuffed in separate police cruisers. And with that, Cwiz learned a critical lesson about the po-po. Cops do not have to tell you the truth, especially if they are interested in arresting you. They will say what they need to say to get you to come willingly, and then sit your ass down in the back of their cruiser.

When the guys arrived at the station, they were all booked on felony terrorism charges. This was before 9/11, but you can imagine how that kind of charge looks on a background check when you're trying to get a job.

In the long run, however, the charges were dropped to misdemeanors and all the boys got off with community service sentences. Many of them later had their records expunged.

LIFE LESSON:

When one of your friends suggests making a bomb—take a pass.

CHAPTER 30

LOOKUPHERE!

Our pal Amir was a student at Biola University, a four-year private Christian school. Because Amir was suddenly plugged into a whole new social pipeline of girls, we started visiting him...a lot. But because we were not students at his school, we were not exactly welcome visitors, from a campus safety perspective. It did not help that one of the first things Cwiz did when we arrived on campus to visit Amir (without his knowing we were coming, by the way) was to climb a massively ancient ficus tree in the middle of the campus plaza.

The tree dominated the plaza and had low-hanging branches that jutted out over a staircase down to a café. The lowest branch hung about eight feet above the top of the stairs that led into the quad, and was thick enough and strong enough for a fully grown man like Cwiz to lie down on it without dipping the branch an inch.

Cwiz climbed up the tree and lay down on the lowest branch, waiting for someone to walk by. As soon as a student distractedly walked underneath him, he hissed like a jaguar and swung a paw, scaring the crap out of them. The student would hold their heart, or drop their books, and freak out. Then they would see us jerks laughing at them in the quad and notice that everyone there was enjoying the jaguar attacks.

Eventually, the Captain, Cory, and I joined Cwiz in the tree, each of us taking a corner of the top for ourselves. At the top, the branches were narrower and swayed in the wind under our weight.

The quad was full of students hurrying from class to class, engaging in conversations, and eating lunch. We started imitating

Steve Martin in *The Three Amigos*. You know, the part where he is trying to get Martin Short's attention by shouting, "Look up here," but doing it with a sort of hooting bird's voice in a way that sounds like a single word.

Cwiz screamed, "*Lookupere!*"

Again and again.

Crowds started to gather underneath us, pointing and laughing. Some of the crowd included cute girls, which was the whole point. But eventually, campus security appeared and started yelling at us to get down.

So we screamed, continuing in bird-like shrieks, "*HowdoIgetdown?*" over and over. Then, the shriek "*Lookuphere*" turned into "*Stuckuphere,*" and the hooting went on and on. The crowd got larger and the laughs louder. The campus security officers, however, were multiplying and not laughing. They did not find this funny at all.

Amir happened to walk by and wonder what all the fuss was about. But as he approached the crowd, he heard our hooting from the tree and knew instantly his friends had come to visit him. Amir walked underneath the tree and told the security guys he would take care of it.

"Hey, guys!"

"Amirrrrrrrrrrrrrr!" we all yelled out.

"Come down before you all get arrested."

We all climbed down and promised never ever to do it again. The security officers let us go. Meanwhile, those in the crowd who knew Amir wanted to know who the tree guys were, and Cwiz got a few dates out of it.

LIFE LESSON:
If you're having trouble finding a date, try drawing a lot of attention to yourself.

Chapter 31

Traffic School

Cwiz had his fair share of driving infractions. He was not slavishly devoted to obeying the speed limit—or any other vehicle code provisions, for that matter. As a result, he found himself obligated to attend traffic school from time to time.

In years past, traffic school typically involved spending an entire Saturday in a classroom auditorium with hundreds of other miserable souls. The school would start early, like 8 a.m., and would usually drag on until 4 p.m., with a fifteen-minute break in the morning, a one-hour lunch period, and then a second fifteen-minute break in the afternoon. It was brutal.

Because every single person in the room already knew how to drive, the entire thing felt like a complete waste of time. This was not education; it was punishment. Telling people the rules of a four-way stop will not prevent them from speeding, but boring them to tears for eight hours on a gorgeous and sunny Saturday just might.

Cwiz was resigned to his punishment on this particular Saturday, but he decided he was going to extract his fun tax. He was going to find a way to redeem his miserable Saturday with an experience that he would never forget. He brainstormed and came up with a plan.

When he arrived, about ten minutes before the start of class, the auditorium was nearly full. Hundreds of people slumped in their chairs, preparing to suffer. Cwiz surveyed the scene from the back of the room and then walked purposefully toward the center stage. He took the podium and saw hundreds of pairs of eyes land on him.

He said, "Good morning, everyone. I'm your instructor today. You can call me Jimmy."

An uncomfortable silence descended on the room, broken only by the shifting of a roomful of strangers in squeaky chairs.

Cwiz continued, "I have some good news for you today. Although these classes normally go until 4 p.m., I actually have a wedding to go to this afternoon. So, my plan is to rush through this material as quickly as I can and get us out of here before noon. Sound good?"

The class suddenly perked up in their seats. Some people started clapping. Various whoops and hollers of delight broke out around the auditorium. A contagious grin spread from stranger to stranger. Cwiz heard someone shout, "Yes!"

Cwiz went on. "I won't tell if you don't, okay? Now I have to get something I forgot in my car. I'll be back in a few, and then we'll get started."

Cwiz walked down the center aisle through the room, savoring the open smiles and excited buzz. He walked out of there like he had just given a State of the Union speech. These people were in love with him.

He walked out the back, went to the restroom, and then snuck back into the classroom, grabbing the last seat in the last row. A guy with a hoodie drawn over his head, one row in front of him, noticed him sitting there.

Hoodie said, "What are you doing?"

Cwiz said, "I'm here to learn, bro."

"But you're the instructor."

Cwiz just shook his head and gave him an evil smirk.

Hoodie said, "Are you serious, dude? That's cold."

Just then, the real instructor came in. He walked down the center of the aisle and took the podium, as Cwiz had done a few minutes before. The instructor said, "Good morning, everyone. My name is Mr. So-and-So. Hopefully all of you picked up the class materials outside. Please raise your hand if you did not get the material."

The class sat mute and confused, until one girl raised her hand.

When the instructor gestured toward her, she said, "Um, I think you must be in the wrong class. Another instructor actually already started the class, but then he had to go get something and he is coming back."

The instructor looked put out. He said, "I'm not sure what you're talking about. Who came in?"

The girl said, "Some guy came in and said he was our instructor today and that we were ending early."

He smiled. "No, I'm afraid not. I am the instructor, and we are going until 4 p.m. today like we always do. Now, do you have your materials, Miss, or not?"

The classroom groaned in agony. One of the students yelled out, "I want the other instructor back."

Meanwhile, Cwiz sank into his chair and whizzed himself with glee, laughing alone, counting the minutes until he could call his buddies and tell them what he did.

LIFE LESSON:
Never underestimate the power of expectation.

CHAPTER 32

HAS THIS BEEN LAUNDERED?

There was a time when I (and pretty much every one of my buddies) was obsessed with *The Late Show with David Letterman*. When we learned he was coming to Los Angeles for a week of taping, Cwiz and I jumped at the chance to see him. I wrote a letter to the show requesting tickets, and amazingly, we got them.

The day of the taping, Cwiz and I drove down to the CBS lot in Los Angeles really early, hours before we were supposed to be there. We figured if we got there early, we might be able to poke around and see something cool. And we were right.

We found the studio parking lot and started driving around for a spot. In the back of the lot, in a gazebo, David Letterman was going over his lines with Tony, his cue card guy, who was also a regular on his show. We could not believe our luck and giddily looked at each other in amazement.

Holy crap, that's Dave right there!

We got out of Cwiz's truck and walked over to Dave.

Dave said, "Welcome to the gazebo, boys!" He held out his arms in welcome.

I excitedly yelled, "Hi, Dave!"

We all shook hands and introduced ourselves, and Dave graciously took a few pictures with us.

Then Cwiz said, "Dave, can you do me one more favor?"

"Well, that depends, Caesar."

"I have this sweatshirt with my face on it. It's sort of a promotional thing. Would you put it on so I can take a picture of you wearing it?"

"Let me see it."

Mortified, I stood there lamely with Dave and Tony while Cwiz ran back to his truck. Cwiz returned with a balled-up sweatshirt that had clearly been stuffed under the seat. On the back of the sweatshirt, there was a large picture of Cwiz, but as a four-year-old boy, wearing a cowboy hat and riding a pony. Under the picture, it said "Coco Cwiz—I Like Cookies."

The sweatshirt was one of the strange things he used to create and give to people for no apparent reason other than rank self-promotion. It is not like he had a business he was promoting at the time; he was just selling himself (the CWIZ!) as some grand idea with T-shirts, sweatshirts, and stickers. He had shirts that said "Coco Cwiz—He Is Not Safe But He Is Good," (a reference to Aslan from *The Chronicles of Narnia*) and others that said "Cwiz Was Here."

Around this same time frame, Cwiz was putting up "Cwiz Was Here" stickers all over the city. If he was inside your house, he would secretly write "Cwiz Was Here" on various household objects—even the cereal boxes. Maybe a month would go by after he was at your house, and then you would turn over a box of cookies and notice he had tagged the box with his name. It was nuts.

Cwiz handed the sweatshirt to Dave.

Dave held it up gingerly, made a confused face at the picture, and asked, "Has this been laundered?"

Cwiz laughed nervously and said, "Yeah, but it's been a while."

Dave said, "I'm not gonna wear it, but how's this?" and he wrapped the sweatshirt over his shoulders, preppy style.

Cwiz snapped the shot and we thanked him profusely and went on our way, giddily replaying what happened until the show started hours later. They say you should never meet your heroes because it usually does not go well, but I loved Dave even more after that experience.

LIFE LESSON:
Love yourself enough to self-promote.

PART THREE

THE ROAMING YEARS

Me (left), the Captain (middle), and Cruz (right) in Santorini, Greece, 1997.

CHAPTER 33

IN ALL HIS GLORY

Y ou might say Cwiz had a sort of exhibitionist phase. Thankfully, the phase passed long ago, peaking around the summer of '97. That summer, Cwiz, the Captain, and I were traveling in Europe. I met Cwiz and the Captain in Athens, Greece, where I was starting my trip. They had already packed in a month of adventure through western Europe without me. I had missed out, but I was ready to start catching up.

After a couple of days in Athens, we made our way to the islands, as young backpackers usually do. While staying at a riotous backpacker camp on the island of Ios, we found ourselves eating breakfast at the pool one morning. Though it was early, it was already very hot. Hundreds of young partygoers were at the pool, and the day-drinking had already begun.

While I dug into my pancakes and wrestled with how to look at a stranger's bare breasts without appearing creepy, Cwiz suddenly stood up without a word, took off his shirt, and walked toward the pool.

I said to Ian, "What's he doing?"

Ian said, "I don't know."

I said, "He's in the middle of his breakfast. Where's he going?"

With a smile, Ian said, "It's his time to shine." The Captain, leaning back in his chair and folding his arms, seemed to know what was coming.

Cwiz walked through the densely packed early-morning pool area, pointing and smiling in the cheesiest way possible at "the ladies," as he always put it. He slowly meandered toward the pool through the groups of Europeans and stepped right up to the edge.

He surveyed his surroundings deliberately, with a very serious look on his face. His toes wiggled over the pool's edge. I knew I was about to be entertained in some memorable way, perhaps in a way I might later write about, but I had no idea at the time what he was going to do.

The pool was shaped like a huge lima bean, and Cwiz stood right in the bean's crease, right at the center of the pool. There were probably fifty people in the pool talking, splashing, and drinking. Hundreds more were lounging around the pool and restaurant area, bobbing their heads to the techno.

Cwiz began playing the part of a lonely business traveler on the prowl. He took on a look of self-satisfaction and arrogance, with pursed lips and one turned-up eyebrow. It was the kind of look where the man puts out the vibe and lingers a little too long in his gaze, hoping some lucky lady will take notice. Cwiz surveyed the pool's occupants in this fashion for a minute.

Finally, Cwiz dipped his toe in the pool right next to two girls who were sitting on the edge, sipping their cocktails. He stretched his arms over his head for some time, first to the left, then to the right. Then he put them both over his head and arched his back, backwards, in a long stretch. He then bent over and touched his toes, letting out a loud moan and pretending it took a great deal of energy to stretch his finely tuned muscles.

What made his little display all the more comical was that Cwiz was not exactly a sculpted machine. He was not fat by any means, but he was a big dude and he enjoyed a plate of cookies now and again. When he started doing his deep knee bends and lunges, and continuing to groan with the effort, everyone around the pool looked up and took notice, and the girls next to him scooched over to get to a comfortable distance.

Then, at the precise moment when the most attention was focused on him, Cwiz decisively dropped his trunks. It was perfectly executed. Ian and I practically fell out of our chairs laughing. After standing in silent naked glory for several seconds, he slowly plucked his feet from his shorts one at a time while standing perfectly erect (his whole body, I mean) and let everyone take it in while he continued stretching.

The girls next to him were trying to duck and cover their heads, and about half of the crowd were laughing and grabbing their friends to look. Then Cwiz dove into the pool like a four-year-old. You know how four year-olds put their hands together on top of their heads, hold the pose, and then fall slowly into the pool in a sort of belly flop, where all parts of the body hit the water at the same time, and yet the kid's hands are still together? Imagine that. Except it's a 200-pound naked dude. Ian and I were in convulsions.

It was going to be a good summer.

LIFE LESSON:
If you've got it, flaunt it.

CHAPTER **34**

THE VOMITFOIL

The three of us were standing on a reeking dock with our heavy backpacks, sweating in the morning sun, waiting to board a hydrofoil from Greece to Selçuk, Turkey. Cwiz dropped his backpack with us and went to the bathroom, leaving Ian and me in line.

Ian said in exasperation, "Dude, I am telling you, he has not had a vegetable of any kind in a month. He exists entirely on flour, cheese, and corn syrup. He eats nothing but margherita pizzas, ice cream, and Coke."

I laughed. "What else is new?"

Ian looked serious. "No man, I'm serious. I have been telling him for a month to eat something real."

"Okay, we'll work on it."

It was obvious these two needed a break from each other. The Captain was right that Cwiz was the pickiest eater in the world, like a kid sometimes. He still is, truth be told. But Ian could push his buttons when it was not necessary. There had sometimes been an uneasy, fragile peace between these two, both seeking to be in charge of any given situation. Ian was the Captain, after all. He was used to calling his own shots, but so was Cwiz. They had a tendency to go at each other like rams dueling for harem rights, but anyone could see that they loved each other like brothers.

My role was to keep these two heading the same direction and to side with whichever one of them wanted to privately complain about the other. It seemed to keep the peace, and we all knew that when we channeled our energies in the same direction, we were capable of epic creativity and fun. It would be no different than it was at home, and in fact, I thought it would be far better. There were so many new experiences to be had overseas, and I could not wait to see what kind of trouble we would get into over the next month.

I watched the hydrofoil rock gently as the passengers climbed on. It looked like a mad scientist's mixture of a boat, snowmobile, jet, and hovercraft, or like some engineer dropped acid and then began contemplating how to ferry huge numbers of people across the Aegean Sea at the speed of sound.

The front of our ship looked like the X-1 jet that Chuck Yeager flew in the movie *The Right Stuff*. You know the jet that broke the sound barrier for the first time? Instead of orange, though, the ship's bow was yellow and blue, came to a sharp point, and was anchored on the surface of the water by huge hanging skis, with suspension rods going into the hull of the ship.

The remainder of the ship angled diagonally downward so that the back of it was nearly underwater, while the front pointed toward the sky. I half expected spinning rims and blaring rap music.

Our seats were in the bow, or the nose of the hydrofoil. The bow was an enclosed space with approximately fifty seats facing forward like an airplane. There were two watertight, steel doors at the rear that led to a walkway outside to the rear cabins. When we sat down, we saw we were smack dab in the middle of a Japanese tour group, matching shirts and all.

The hydrofoil's steel deck shuddered as it powered up. As the ship motored out of the harbor and picked up speed, the nose lifted toward the sky. We were thrown back in our seats. *We have lift-off.*

In the bow, each of the passengers had their own airplane-style seat, complete with seat belts and vomit bags. It was a good thing too, because the foil really started rocking and bouncing over the waves on its suspended skis once we cleared the harbor. I could not see the water at all, only spray and clouds through the tiny windows, which were facing skyward. Through the tiny portholes, the clouds were jumping up and down as the ship was slipping and sliding across the water.

The sensation of riding in a hydrofoil is nothing like riding in a ferry or any other kind of boat. The front of the boat is literally riding on skis over the water at an incredible speed. As far as I could tell, the sole ambition of the hydrofoil captain is to transfer all of his passengers to the destination before they puke. The problem is that the faster the hydrofoil goes, the less likely it is that the captain will succeed.

It was not long before some of the Japanese folks around us started reaching for their vomit bags, clutching them in their laps and looking frightened through their tinted facemasks. I saw the little lady across the aisle from me look behind her nervously, presumably searching for a toilet, and I started to get nervous myself. I imagined what our capsule would smell like once these people lost it.

I bumped Cwiz next to me and pointed out all of the bag-clutching going on. He had been too busy hooting and hollering over every major wave and bump, laughing with Ian. When he noticed that 90 percent of our new friends were about to have their lunch for a second time, he started making loud, disgusting guttural noises—the kind of noises people make when they puke.

Cwiz mimicked puking noises: "Hoooaaaahhhhkkk, haaaaooooooaaahhhggkkkk."

He made the noise over and over again, as loud as he could.

The people in the rows in front of us bowed their heads, several more people reached for their own bags and then ... the real stuff started flowing. The little Japanese lady across from me unleashed a torrent of porridge into her bag. Before we knew it, people were puking all over the place, and the smell of oily feta and fish filled the cabin.

Cwiz was red-eyed and cackling with laughter when he sprang up out of his chair to get out of the room to avoid the smell. Ian and I jumped up with him to get some fresh air, bracing ourselves in the aisle by holding the chairs of our puking Japanese brethren as the cabin bucked.

We stumbled toward the heavy metal door using our hands on the seats to help us balance, with Cwiz leading the way, when the vomitfoil lurched forward unexpectedly. Cwiz fell backwards, all his weight landing on the back of a Japanese dude's chair. The chair folded forward under the pressure of Cwiz's large frame, the guy's head flung into his own lap, and for a second the poor man disappeared into a chair sandwich.

Cwiz got his footing as the ship righted itself, but he was now beyond hysteria. He tried to say sorry through his frenzied laughter and tears, and stumbled out the door with us following, all of us wiping tears from our eyes and giggling like children.

We finally got to the steel door and opened it to get outside, and as soon as we did, a massive wave came out of nowhere and blasted our walkway, utterly soaking the three of us. It was as if a dumpster-sized bucket of water were thrown at us by a sea giant at point-blank range. We looked at each other, shocked, spit the ocean foam from our mouths, and laughed even harder at how ridiculous this stinking hydrofoil was.

LIFE LESSON:
Never eat a gyro before an ocean voyage.

CHAPTER 35

HAVE YOU EVER BEEN IN A TURKISH PRISON?

Cwiz was broke, hurt, and alone…in Turkey.

He was broke because the geniuses at the bank, thinking someone had stolen his credit card, put a freeze on it, and he could not access any more cash. He was alone because the Captain and I, being the good friends that we were, said "Sucks for you" and told him to get his business squared away. Then the Captain and I took off to Cappadocia to see more cool stuff without Cwiz. We told him we would meet him in Istanbul in a few days (assuming he could get there).

Now broke and alone but still healthy (two out of three ain't bad), he stopped at a travel agent's office and booked the cheapest means of transportation he could find to get himself to Istanbul—a cheap bus to Gemlik and then a second bus from there to Istanbul. But after he purchased the tickets to Gemlik, he still had to get to the main terminal in Selçuk.

He found a city bus that would get him to the main terminal, and with his backpack strapped to his waist, and pulling him backward from its weight, he hopped on and pushed his way through the locals to the back of the bus. There was nowhere to sit, and very little standing room, so he found a spot in the back stairwell. The swiveling rear door was broken and remained open during the ride.

Cwiz was standing just above the gears of the swiveling door on the top step. Because he was still wearing his unwieldy backpack, he was shifting from side to side during the long ride, trying to get comfortable. While he was adjusting his waistbelt with both hands, suddenly, the bus jerked and threw him down the stairwell and toward the open doorway. To keep himself from flying face first onto the moving pavement, he threw out his arms and legs, flailing for a hold. His hand caught a rail, but his foot jammed itself into the gears of the swiveling door. He managed to stay in the bus, but it cost him. His big toe was impaled in the gears and was already bleeding profusely.

At the next stop, he got off and, showing a passerby his toe, was led to an emergency room of sorts where they stitched him up, wrapped the toe, and deprived him of nearly all of his remaining cash.

After limping into the main terminal, he hucked his backpack into the bowels of the bus to Gemlik for his first leg of the trip to Istanbul and took a window seat. As soon as the bus fired up and rolled out of the parking lot, a vague sorrow started to fill the edges of his mind. This was a foreign feeling for him. He looked out the window at nothing in particular and gave in to the wretchedness rolling in like a thunderstorm.

By the time he got to the town of Gemlik and learned that he would have to wait nearly all day for the bus to Istanbul to depart, he was disconsolate. He limped slowly to a plaza and found a place to sit. His bag was too painful to carry, so he managed to convince a woman who appeared to live at the plaza to take his bag into her house and keep it there for the day.

Without his bag, he could walk a little better, but every step was still painful. He found a place to sit on the outer wall of a fountain in the plaza, and looked at his toe, now bleeding through the bandages.

Loneliness fell on him, sinking his shoulders and collapsing him as he sat. As locals went about their business, he stifled a desire to cry in public.

But after a time, he mastered his emotion. He limped over to the edge of the plaza to buy a Coke and sat in a restaurant waiting out the long day until his next bus. He watched a happy young couple walk by and felt a sour pang of jealousy. He saw a family walk past. The dad was carrying his daughter on his shoulders with a smile on his face. And in a moment of sudden inspiration, Cwiz pulled out some paper and a pen from his daypack and started to write a letter. He wrote the letter slowly and thoughtfully, measuring each word. When he was finished writing it, he neatly stuffed it in his pack. The letter traveled with him the rest of the trip and was never mailed.

When he got home from overseas many weeks later, he put the letter in an envelope and addressed the envelope to no specific person. He then placed the letter in a plastic storage bin in the back of his closet. That letter was the only thing in the bin.

Cwiz miraculously found the Captain and me at a bus terminal when we pulled into Istanbul on a bus from Cappadocia the following day. After several days of tooling around Istanbul, we had to catch a flight to Tel Aviv. Our plan was to leave the country without a single Turkish lyra to spare. We pooled our remaining funds and counted it up. We had 6 million lyra, which sounded like a lot, but it wasn't.

We hoped to negotiate with a taxi driver to take us to the airport for the remaining 6 million lyra so that we wouldn't have to exchange any more money. For the next week, we would be in Israel, and it would be shekels for us from now on.

We walked around with our packs for a little bit, looking for a cabby who seemed desperate for a fare. We found this sleepy cabby somewhat close to the Blue Mosque and explained to him several hundred times that 6 million lyra was all we had. We showed him the money in hand.

We said, "Six million lyra for airport. That's it."

He nodded without a word.

We said it again, sticking the money at him. "That's all. Six million." We even turned out our pockets to show we had no more money.

He said, "Okay," which I think was his only English word.

I said, "Really, this is all you're gonna get."

He looked at me in a way that meant, *Okay, seriously, bro, I'm gonna punch you. I get it.*

So we relented and got in.

We threw our bags in the trunk, and the cabby tore out of the parking lot like one of us was giving birth, which didn't seem consistent with how sleepy he appeared.

We exchanged frightened looks and between moments of sheer terror and gasping, I noticed that the meter was already at 6 million lyra. During the ride to the airport, which turned out to be really long, we exchanged nervous looks. We knew the cabby was going to squawk for more money no matter what we said or did. When we saw airplanes slowly gliding in their approach overhead, we knew we were close.

The Captain whispered, "When he stops, let's get our bags out first, put 'em on, then we'll give him the cash and bail."

The cab rolled into the unloading area of the international terminal, stopped, and we quickly hopped out. The cabby sauntered out, opened the trunk casually, and waited while we strapped on our backpacks.

When we were properly girded, the Captain handed him the 6 million lyra, we turned as one unit in a choreographed about-face, and we beelined for the terminal.

A shriek rang out behind us. It sounded like our cabby had just been gored by a bull. We did not turn around.

I could hear his footsteps coming behind us, but we were "eyes forward" the whole time. We moved ahead toward the automatic terminal doors, somehow believing that if we could just get inside those doors, the cabby would be magically prevented from entering.

The cabby grabbed Cwiz's pack and whipped him around. He got in his face, screaming who knows what and waving the 6 million lyra over his head. Cwiz shed his grip and the three of us picked up our pace, almost running to the terminal.

The cabby was not dissuaded. He followed us into the terminal, shouting and trying to get the attention of those around him.

Of course, by this time, there was no avoiding it. We were in the middle of a full-blown international incident now. Although we tried to pretend there was not a lunatic behind us, cursing us to his fellow countrymen in the terminal, there was a growing sense that the Turks were closing in. We were not going to make it to security. He was not going to go away.

And then I saw a group of soldiers—carrying machine guns and bayonets—turn toward us and then rush over. My first thought was the line delivered by the pilot in the movie *Airplane*: "Joey, have you ever been in a Turkish prison?"

You'd be surprised at how fast you sit when the business end of a bayonet is pointing at your gullet. We dropped to our butts and sat in a position reminiscent of three-year-olds during story time.

The cabby continued yelling, this time to the soldiers, while he pointed at us. There was a lot of wild gesturing going on, and we sat there mutely. One of the soldiers tried to reason with him and calm him down, but he wasn't having it, which worked in our favor, because the soldiers started to get annoyed.

One of the big ones moved over to the cabby, pushed his smaller, more diplomatic soldier buddy aside, and said something to the cabby that made him re-evaluate his position. I don't know what he said, but the cabby became as compliant as we were.

Then the diplomatic one came to me, knelt down, and asked in plain English what happened. Cwiz explained to him we negotiated a deal with the cabby and that he agreed to 6 million lyra for the trip to the airport, but that when we arrived, this crazy guy refused to stick to our deal, that he wanted more.

That was all he needed to hear. He stood up and said something to the cabby that I interpreted to mean, *Get out of here, jackass.*

The cabby glared at us, turned on his heel, and left.

Cwizzy turned to us and said, "Well, that was nearly a very cool story."

LIFE LESSON:
Get it in writing.

Chapter 36

Egyptian Brawl

The Sinai is a slice-of-pizza-shaped slab of land, a barrier, that exists between Israel and Egypt. And on the right side of this pizza slice, on the southeast coast, lies the sluggish little town of Dahab. We had made our way down to Dahab after a week in Israel.

Our lodging in Dahab was a thatched-roof hut, fifty yards from the shore of the Gulf of Aqaba in the Red Sea. The room's amenities were as follows: three floor mats and a door. That's it. The bathroom was across a dirt road. Our door, which was wood slats shoddily strapped together with wire, was too short. There was a foot of space on top of the door for you to look outside (and for someone to look in) and a foot of space on the bottom, which explains how I woke up looking at a chicken.

I was entering that half-conscious place, where the conscious part of you starts taking what you're hearing and incorporating it into your dream. I heard some weird scratching noises, very quiet, but close to my ear. In my dream, Frankenstein was raking leaves, and his raking perfectly aligned with the scratching next to my ear. I rolled over, opened my eyes, and came face to face with this scraggly chicken, who was scratching the ground with shriveled claws.

It perked up, gave me that fight or flight look, and appeared to be thinking, *Okay, is he going to kill me or feed me? I'll just stand here for a second and look at him sideways until I'm sure.*

I laughed, and it bolted under the space in the bottom of the door to sift through the dirt somewhere else. My laughter woke up Cwiz and the Captain, and we all got up to hunt for breakfast.

All the activity in the little Egyptian town of Dahab focused on its shimmering crescent bay. The dwellings and storefronts were all seemingly within twenty-five yards of shore, smashed up against the Red Sea's mild waves.

Lining the entire shorefront, bustling restaurants vied for customers. But "restaurant" isn't really the right word, because these eateries did not have any chairs, tables, or even walls. Instead, they welcomed us with mats, blankets, and pillows thrown on the ground right next to the water, which was held at bay by a breaker. Palm trees shaded the mats, strings of Christmas lights were suspended between the trees, and ratty tarps were tied up here and there for shade.

At 8 a.m., it was already easily 100 degrees. Dahab is in the Sinai Desert, after all, and we happened to be there in August. It would be over 120 degrees by the end of the day, as it was every day in August.

So we picked a place that we reckoned had the best shade. Pillows were arranged in groups around tiny stools, with napkins and menus on top. People ate chocolate pancakes, lounging sideways on their elbows, on the ground.

We picked a spot on the ground without being greeted by anyone and lay there looking at the water through the frame of our bare feet for about half an hour. I had been coaxed back to sleep by the rhythm of the waves when a young Egyptian man with very dark skin and a coruscating smile appeared.

He said, "Bonjour," and handed us three menus.

We said, "Hello," and he responded, "Something to drink?"

A half hour later, he appeared again with a Coke for Cwiz and the nastiest orange juice you could possibly imagine for Ian and me. It tasted like tangerine Kool-Aid with chunks of beef in it. Then, probably another half hour after that, he came back and asked us if we wanted anything to eat.

As I was looking over the menu, I noticed some strange items on the back with names I could not identify. It wasn't exactly unusual to be confused, being in Egypt and all. But the confusing terms were in English, and I couldn't make out what they meant. Terms like Ganga Green, Hustler Hash, and Electric Rasta. While I puzzled over this, I smelled something familiar and noticed some backpackers behind us smoking pot.

"We're all going to have the banana pancakes," said Ian.

The waiter said, "Any bud?"

"What?" said Ian.

"Bud?"

"No, thanks," said Ian, and the waiter walked off.

"What'd he say?" said Ian.

"Dude," I said. "Pot is on the menu."

"No way."

"Look." I pointed to the Coconut Blunt on the menu. "And check out the dudes behind us."

"Holy crap," said Cwiz.

"You can't buy a beer in Egypt, but you can buy weed?" I said.

"Don't ask questions," said Cwiz.

The meal took about three hours, but the banana pancakes were worth every second. We learned right away that this was not the kind of place that forgave being in a hurry. You were forced to relax because there was not much to do, and even if you asked someone to help you do something, it'd still take hours before it happened.

I was completely relaxed after one half-day of lying around in the shade. I strategically placed myself under the shifting shade of a single palm leaf and lay there in my sweaty T-shirt, watching the endless procession of waves beating on the shore, existing halfway between sleeping and waking for hours on end throughout the day.

Every so often, a slow-walking Egyptian, in only a white robe and sandals, would walk by on the sand in front of the waves, leading four or five camels linked by a single rope, going who knows where and doing who knows what.

This was the Platonic form of relaxation. Even the chickens seemed to be chillin' out, pecking the crumbs around my feet slower than other chickens do.

Finally bored, we went for a snorkel. We hitched a ride in the bed of a small pickup truck over to a dive site called the Blue Hole. We rented some snorkel gear and spent the afternoon frolicking in the water, drying off in the sun within thirty seconds and running back into the water to avoid heat stroke. The entire day pretty much went like this:

"Let's snorkel."

"Sounds good."

Once we got in the water: "Bbbb Bbbaaaa, bbbaa boo."

"What?"

"Bbbb Bbbaaaa, bbbaa boo."

"Stop trying to talk through your snorkel, moron."

"Okay, but we'll need hand signals."

"We're not Delta Force. We're not using hand signals."

"Let's get out. I'm tired."

Once we were out of the water: "I'm dry already. Sheesh."

"How long have we been out of the water?"

"Like five minutes. Let's get back in. It's too hot out here."

"Dude, did you see that lionfish? I think they're poisonous, so keep your distance."

[Repeat fifty times.]

On our way back from the Blue Hole, Cwiz had to go to the bank. We caught a ride in the bed of another pickup truck on the way back to town. The driver agreed to drop us off at this bank, which was off the beaten path (literally B.F.E.), but where he said we could do "international banking."

Cwiz had to go to a bank with international capability because his credit card was still shut down after all this time. Cwiz had been trying to get through to the bank for a couple weeks now to release his funds, and he was down to his last few dollars. I walked into the bank with him, and he explained the situation as best he could to the bank manager, who allowed him to use the phone to call his bank in the States. After about five minutes, he was disconnected.

I was milling around the bank, not doing anything in particular during his telephone call, when I noticed that Cwiz and the bank manager were in a heated exchange.

"You must pay $14 for the phone call now."

"I don't have $14," Cwiz said.

"You called America," said the bank manager, looking perplexed.

Cwiz was pleading, "You don't understand. The bank in the United States froze my card. I have nothing left until I can get the bank to release the hold they put on my cards. That's why I was calling the US."

"Fourteen dollars."

Cwiz turned around and looked at me helplessly. So did the bank manager.

The manager pointed at me and said, "He can pay $14."

Cwiz walked over to me, out of earshot of the manager. "Are you hearing this? Can you pay it?"

I said, "No, I'm nearly as broke as you. I'll go outside and wait with the taxi."

Cwiz said, "Okay, get the cabby ready and tell him to pull up to the bank."

As soon as we pulled up, Cwiz came flying out the front doors of the bank. Cwiz jumped into the bed of the truck at full speed, and the pickup took off down the dusty road.

Cwiz was now a broke fugitive in Egypt with a jacked-up toe.

The following morning, while we were scarfing down what must have been our fifteenth plate of hot bananas since we arrived, we heard someone yelling in Arabic behind us, which was not unusual. We witnessed public screaming in one form or another on a daily basis; it appeared the people in that part of the world were more comfortable expressing their feelings publicly than we were.

We turned toward the restaurant, and there, on the dirt road directly behind us, was our waiter, who was about twenty-five years of age, yelling at a younger man of perhaps eighteen. The younger man had his head down and appeared resigned to taking the abuse—that is, until our waiter reached back and slapped him in the face. The young man was shocked and reeling a bit from the blow, but before he could do anything, a huge dude in a tank top, whom I took to be the cook, came running out of the restaurant, screaming at the top of his lungs.

This is where it gets weird. The cook grabbed both of them by the neck and started yelling at them. Then a fourth dude, an older guy in a robe, came from behind the guy who got slapped, shoved him away from the fracas as if to protect him, and started yelling at the cook and at our waiter (the slapper).

So now we've got four hyped-up dudes screaming at each other. Things are getting out of hand. All the customers swiveled completely around on our pillows to watch the action. There was finally something to watch besides the waves.

Then somebody must have said something about somebody's mama, because suddenly the four of them stopped shouting and started looking around like, "Oh, no, he didn't!"

The slappee suddenly took off into the next-door neighbor's house, which was right next to the restaurant. Within seconds, he came back out, walking with a slow determination and a crazy look in his eye. He was pointing a machete at the waiter.

Holy crap! Our waiter is going to die.

Our waiter wasn't going to go down easy, though. He ran into the restaurant and came out with a huge metal fencepost, 4 feet long and 3 inches in diameter. It looked like it weighed 50 pounds. He raised his weapon up and went right at the slappee. When the two maniacs got within 10 feet of each other, the screaming in Arabic reached a crescendo, until they were suddenly mauled by a huge group of people. I had no idea where all of these people came from. It was like they were hidden in the trees, at the ready for such an eventuality. In one moment, there were four dudes there who were going to kill each other, and in the next moment, there were twenty-five Egyptians breaking up the fight with expert skill.

I saw one of the peacemakers wrestle the machete out of the hands of the slappee, who was being held by the mysterious ones, and walk it back into the house. Our waiter had also been manhandled, de-weaponed, and sent to his corner.

As quickly as they had come, all of these people vanished, and the combatants went about their business. It seemed choreographed. The silence of the waves was back. The backpackers all looked at each other, completely dumbfounded.

As if nothing had happened, our waiter walked over to us and said, "Can I get you anything else?"

LIFE LESSON:
Let bygones be bygones.

CHAPTER 37

BABOON BRAWL

Have you ever witnessed a troop of primate burglars fight your best friend? Ever lanced your infected toe while sitting on a giant tortoise? Ever run from gunfire alongside a police officer in a riotous city? No, you say? Well, Cwiz has done all of these things, and all within forty-eight hours.

Cwiz and the Captain were in Africa—Kenya, to be exact. To my deep disappointment, I went home after our time together in Egypt, while the two of them caught a flight to Nairobi and adventured without me. Once in Nairobi, they immediately hoofed it to the Masai Mara for a safari, where they drove around in Jeeps and slept in tents in the wilderness. They gawked with glee at elephants, rhinos, hippos, lions, and giraffes.

At night, they gathered around a campfire under a canopy and swapped stories with the guides and the other tourists. In such places and at such times, Cwiz and the Captain were unrivaled in their storytelling, no doubt telling some of the stories in this book.

"Remember the trial of OJ Simpson? Well, have I got a story for you...."

One night while the group of about a dozen tourists was sitting around the campfire, the Captain went to their two-person tent to fetch something. While walking back to the fire from the tent, Cwiz turned around and saw that Ian had failed to zip up the tent—something they had been repeatedly told they must do.

Their bush guide, Kinga, had emphasized this. Kinga said, "You must close your tents and keep them closed at all times. The baboons will take all your things if you do not do this."

Ian did not do this.

To hear Cwiz tell it, Ian failed to zip up the tent for the umpteenth time, and Cwiz was tired of telling him to do it. Cwiz watched him walk away from the tent again and not zip it up.

Jesus, this guy was an Eagle Scout, thought Cwiz.

Just as Cwiz was about to tell him to go back and zip it up, and while Ian was walking away from the tent, a waist-high eighty-pound primate shot into the tent like a lightning bolt. The baboon had apparently been waiting for the opportunity.

Cwiz started screaming at Ian, "Dude! There's a monkey in the tent!"

When Ian turned around to look, he saw the baboon exit the tent, nonchalant. In his tensile hand, the baboon held Ian's backpack. To be specific, the thief was holding Ian's daypack, which had his camera, journal, some snacks, and, most significantly for Ian, his passport!

For the briefest of moments, Ian froze, unsure of how to proceed, being unclear on the rules of engagement with lesser primates. It was smaller than him, but standing at half Ian's size and baring its intimidating fangs, claws, and its red ass, this little dude caused some understandable anxiety.

The baboon's calculating eyes sized Ian up, and then it took off. It ran for the forest wall, straight for freedom. But Ian, standing closer to the forest wall, ran to cut him off and succeeded in doing so. Ian now blocked the baboon from escape and the baboon stopped, clutching his canvas backpack to his tiny chest with both hands. The baboon appeared to be thinking: *If I'm holding it, it's mine, so back off!*

Ian threw out his arms wide, in order to prevent any sideways escape, and stepped toward the baboon. As soon as he made this threatening gesture, six more pissed-off baboons suddenly materialized out of the forest and surrounded Ian, ready to do him harm. Ian says it was more like twenty of them, and he thought he was going to die. He imagined the big male's fangs sinking into his gut and ripping out his deliciously nutritious innards.

When he looked toward Cwizzy for help, Cwiz carped, "I told you to zip up the tent, man!"

The Captain, sensing an imminent attack, bared his own teeth and hissed at the troop as he spun around to gauge his level of danger. He felt a funneling of his mind, a reduction of his decision-making to primitive instinct. The Captain was the evolutionary product of millions of years of primates dueling over things far less significant than a passport. It was on!

The Captain hissed, "Drop it, punk!"

He was about to die in a spectacularly bitchin' manner. I mean, you can only hope for as cool a story as that when you die, right?

What happened to Ian?

Oh, the Captain? He got into a bare-knuckle jungle brawl with a troop of baboons. Yeah, they ripped him apart and ate him alive.

Oh man, rough way to go.

Yeah, at least he went out doing what he loves, right?

But before the brawl could begin, one of the fellow tourists, an Aussie rugby player named Craigers, jumped up to join this *Planet of the Apes* re-enactment. As he ran toward the encircling baboons, he chucked empty beer bottles in all directions, which scattered several of the baboon gang. Then Craigers heroically tackled the thief, bowling him over on the ground. The backpack dropped free, and the baboon thief ran for the forest wall, followed by the rest of his troop, hooting as they went.

Cwiz grabbed the pack and handed it back to Ian. Then he said, "Zip. Up. The. Tent."

The Captain's eyes were flashing with adrenaline. "Dude, that was amazing though, right?"

Cwiz's jacked-up toe had been a problem for him ever since that bus on the way to Istanbul. The wound was limiting his mobility and also distressing him with its ugliness. He was unable to keep the toe clean as he trudged through the dirt for weeks in Teva sandals, and it became infected. While on the safari, his limp became more exaggerated as the toe squealed at him. He complained to the Captain, and it was overheard by one of their safari members, a lady named Jen who happened to have some medical training.

Jen said, "Let me take a look at it."

Cwiz unwrapped the toe and exposed it in the light of the campfire. It was double the size of a normal toe, puffy and discolored.

Jen said, "You really need to lance this thing. Come on over to my tent."

Cwiz limped over and sat on a fair-sized boulder next to her tent. Jen came out with an alcohol pad and a needle. She started wiping the toe and just as she stabbed it, Cwiz's seat started to move.

Cwiz hopped up on one leg. "What the?"

The boulder was not a boulder, but the hugest tortoise he had ever seen. It was slowly walking away, apparently annoyed that its back was being used as a surgery table. And that is how you end up getting your infected toe lanced while sitting on a massive tortoise.

A day later, Cwiz and the Captain found themselves in Nairobi. The timing could not have been worse. There was tribal unrest in Mumbasa, and refugees were pouring into Nairobi. At the same time, the water supply somehow went offline, and soon, the city was a riotous mêlée.

They were staying at a cheap hostel near the city center. When they went out and walked around the streets to try to find something to eat, they found themselves among throngs of people. There was an eerie, electric energy to the crowds. Everywhere they looked, they saw frightened people, eyes voicing desperation.

Finding no available food anywhere, they kept walking, and soon found themselves in the thick of a full-scale riot. Gunshots could be heard. A limp body lay in the street. Scattered forms ran from doorway to doorway.

A cop stood warily on the corner, talking into his radio. They carefully approached him to ask where they could get some food and get back to their hostel room. As they got near him, a bullet ricocheted off the wall near their heads.

The cop turned to them, visibly shaken, and said, "Now is the time to run."

The three of them ran.

They ran all the way back to the hostel. In the small room they had booked, with the unflushed toilet smell from a stranger filling the room, Ian held up his mother's credit card to Cwiz and said, "Time to break the emergency glass, dude. Let's get out of here."

That night they slept at the Hilton and hid inside the hotel for several days, until they caught a flight out of the city.

When Cwiz finally returned home after several months overseas, he took out two elephant figurines that he had purchased in Nairobi. He turned them over in his hand for a little while and smiled at them. Then he carefully packed them in bubble wrap, taped them up, and placed them gingerly in the plastic storage bin in the back of his closet, along with the letter he wrote in Turkey.

LIFE LESSON:
You can pack a lot of life into forty-eight hours.

CHAPTER **38**

SOUTHEAST ASIA

When Cwiz was eighteen, he met Travis, a twelve-year-old dude at church, whom he would later mentor. Travis was his disciple, literally, during all those formative years, and Trav ate it all up, swallowing whole hog Cwiz's general approach to life. Cwiz's influence, according to Trav, was second only to his parents'.

Like Cwiz, Trav is a force of nature. When he blows into a room, it is all sound and flailing limbs. And like Cwiz, even though Trav is a seriously responsible and successful person (currently a fire captain running a firehouse), he does not let that get in the way of making an ass of himself once in a while. Having thoroughly soaked in Cwiz's life lessons from a young age, Trav is always looking for ways to have a seriously good time.

For years, Cwiz had been encouraging Trav to think big about the world, to go out and see it. When Cwiz, the Captain, and I were traveling together years before, Cwiz would periodically run off to a phone booth with a handful of coins (this was 1997), saying he had to call Trav. Cwiz's crackling voice would come through: "Bro, I'm on a Greek island in the Cyclades. I just dropped trou at our hotel pool in Ios. Look it up. Then think about how you will get yourself here someday!" Cwiz also sent Trav a postcard from Italy. The front depicted a bubbling hot pizza. On the back of the card, it only said, "The pizza is better here—Cwiz." These tiny little acts of inspiration lit a fire in Trav, and he was dying to see the world.

Several years after Cwiz was in Europe and Africa, he teamed up with Travis for a five-week trip around Southeast Asia, including Hong Kong, Singapore, Thailand, and Vietnam. I imagine that part of the world bracing itself for chaos when it found out they were coming, as if two simultaneous hurricanes were descending on the area at the same time.

Cwiz and Trav boarded a plane to Hong Kong the day after Christmas. Trav had just turned twenty-two, and this was the long-promised trip of the teacher and the student. They had talked for years about the trip they would one day take together. It was finally happening. The life lessons Cwiz had been teaching Trav during his formative years about travel and having a good time (all the time) would now be fleshed out in real time, over five weeks, in a trip through Southeast Asia.

After a brief stop in Hong Kong, Trav and Cwiz made their way to Singapore, where they spent four days. There was a family from the church who had coincidentally just moved to Singapore. They were not exactly tight with them, but one of the kids was a student in the high school group where Trav and Cwiz were both high school leaders. Cwiz thought it would be funny to show up unannounced to say hi and blow this kid's mind.

Cwiz got the address from the church secretary, but that was the only thing they had—not even a telephone number. There was no way to call ahead, but Cwiz thought it would be better this way. Better to just show up, he said.

So they spent an entire day on several trains, then several buses, and finally a small motorcycle cab to get to the house. They rapped on the door. Nothing. So they left a note: *"Hey, how's it going. Cwiz and Trav stopped by to say hello. Later."*

On the way back, Trav said, "That was a lot of work."

But Cwiz was giddy about it. "Think about it, dude. Just imagine his face when he sees the note."

For Cwiz, it was about the gift he was leaving: the gift of a funny story. He loved to do stuff that puzzled people. When it did not make a lot of sense, even better.

Cwiz and Trav made their way to Vietnam. When they arrived in Ho Chi Minh City and exited the terminal, they saw a narrow corridor with a chain-link fence on either side. In every hectagonal link of the fence, wiry fingers groped and anxious faces peered at them, some of the faces yelling at them in Vietnamese. Taxi drivers desperate for a fare and hotel owners trying to fill a vacancy were screaming at these impossibly tall Westerners to come with them.

"Nice hotel for you."

A hand reached through the fence and grabbed Trav's backpack. He pulled away.

Trav said, "Dude, this is pure chaos."

Cwiz nodded. "We're not dealing with this. Eyes forward and don't look back."

They set their faces like stone, pushed through the crowd as if they knew exactly where they were going, and walked a full half mile from the airport down a busy road. They were eventually left alone, with several of the hungry hawkers throwing a hand at them in disgust and walking away. They found a lonely taxi driver relaxing at an outdoor café and asked him for a ride. He was happy to oblige.

They picked a hotel next to a construction site downtown. The entire city seemed to be under construction, and the sound of jackhammers was the most prominent sound in the city, blasting like machine guns over the whining of a thousand mopeds.

When they walked into the hotel lobby, the first thing they saw was a dirty fishbowl on the lobby counter. Inside the bowl was a fighting betta fish looking depressed and torn up, apparently from a recent fight with another fish.

Trav looked at Cwiz and pointed at the fish. "Well, that really sets the tone, doesn't it?"

They did not have much of a plan on where to go or what to see in HCM. Luckily, they fell in with two guys who were selling time on their "cyclos." A cyclo is an old rusty bike with a wicker basket on the handlebars that you can sit inside. An adult human man can actually sit in one of these weird baskets and ride around like he's E.T. getting pedaled through the sky by Elliot on Halloween night.

These cyclo drivers flail around the city, pick people up, and taxi them around for next to nothing, and their passengers are hood ornaments as they barrel into the most insane traffic circles you can possibly imagine. The "intersections" have no rules. There are no lights. It is every man for himself. Hundreds of motorbikes, cars, cyclos, and regular bicycles all vie for right-of-way at the same time. Many of the motorbikes are loaded with entire families, with helmetless children sitting stone-faced as they pass by. It appeared to Trav and Cwiz to be unworkable chaos, but to the people of HCM city, this was just another day.

Cwiz found the two cyclo drivers looking bored on a street corner and struck up a conversation with them. In no time, he learned that they were former fighter pilots for the South Vietnamese Air Force. Cwiz, who really liked—and for some reason, trusted—these guys, hired them for the week. The cyclos began to feel protective of Trav and Cwiz and showed them around HCM, dealing with anyone who tried to hassle them. Cwiz joked that he had hired bodyguards for the week.

So that he could find his cyclos easily in a crowd, Cwiz bought four Argentina soccer jerseys from a roadside T-shirt store, and all four of them wore the jerseys every day. Every morning when Trav and Cwiz exited their hotel, there were the cyclos in white- and baby-blue-striped jerseys, with smiles on their faces.

On New Year's Eve, the cyclos knew just where to take Trav and Cwiz for festivities. They dropped them off at a large and loud open plaza. A stage flanked one end of the square, with car-sized speakers strewn up with cables above the plaza stage. A boy band was on stage, gyrating and singing, to the frantic delight of the crowd. Thousands of locals milled about, eating, drinking, and dancing.

And into this black-haired sea of five-foot-tall people walked two dudes in colorful Argentina soccer jerseys, each several inches above six feet tall. Their heads jutted above the surface like whales spy-hopping in kelp beds. Trav and Cwiz could feel the palpable weight of thousands of curious eyes focused on them as they wandered into the crowd and posted up right in the middle of the dancing mass. Trav turned around and located their jersey-wearing cyclo friends, maybe fifty yards behind them, keeping watch.

They found themselves moving in unison with the crowd. They could hardly keep from doing so, packed as tightly as they were. The crowd immediately around them started playfully pawing at them. They weren't sure whether this was a pickpocket attempt at first, but they were being poked and prodded by unseen hands. Then it appeared to them that this wasn't theft, but drunken, playful attempts to entice them into some sort of game.

A small twentysomething dude poked Trav, giggled, and ran toward his friends. Trav spun around yelling, "Hey!" The crowd backed up a little, and someone else poked Cwiz from behind. Suddenly, Trav and Cwiz found themselves in the middle of some sort of gladiator arena where there were two gladiators and 5,000 tiny lions.

Cwiz was now lit up with the hyperactive manic energy of the crowd. A game was afoot, and he was an expert at this sort of tomfoolery. He playfully assumed the form of a grizzly. He hunched over, held both arms in front of him, and loudly growled and yowled at the crowd. He then started chasing those nearest to him as though he were going to eat them, roaring playfully like the hairy bear that he was. The Vietnamese ran from him like they were five-year-old kids playing at home with a crazy, fun uncle. They ran out of his reach and giggled, falling into the crowd.

Suddenly, one of these brave souls snuck up behind the bear and poked him in the butt. Cwiz wheeled around and seized him by the arm. The man was probably about Cwiz's age, perhaps late twenties, but he was no more than 100 pounds. Cwiz picked him up entirely off the ground and military-pressed him up into the air like a professional wrestler, the man cackling in the air above him. Cwiz let out a primal roar and hurled the man headlong into the crowd. The man flew into the mêlée and was caught by a dozen uplifted hands, disappearing into the crowd.

Another volunteer sprang forward. Cwiz grabbed him too, lifted him up, and cannonballed him to the other side. Cwiz had done this innumerable times with his friends' kids in the pool. He could do this all day.

Trav stepped back and watched this spectacle. It was a circus. This went on for several minutes, as Cwiz threw one after another into the crowd. Trav danced and laughed at the nuttiness of it all.

Then the vibe abruptly changed. Cwiz was getting tired, and the crowd was getting more aggressive. One of the guys ran up to the bear and swatted him—hard. Trav saw that the man was not smiling. It was not playful anymore. Cwiz turned around, and the guy was gone. Another person poked him harder, and it hurt.

Trav looked around at the circle of people around the bear and could see the faces turn from generosity to animosity. Cwiz too felt the crowd's collective energy suddenly turn menacing. They were no longer interested in good clean fun. Cwiz shot a look at Trav.

Trav yelled over the music to Cwiz. "Dude, this is getting out of control."

The crowd pressed in, smashing them together.

Cwiz said, "We need to get out of here. Like now."

A guy wrapped his arms around Cwiz's waist. Cwiz pried off the wiry arms and hucked him into the crowd. They started trying to press through the throng, but it wasn't moving. Fear started to take hold.

Just then, behind them, they heard screeching, angry voices over the mob and turned around. The cyclos, clad in those same blessed blue- and white-striped jerseys, were parting the crowd, pushing and shoving anyone standing in their way. They grabbed Trav and Cwiz and started pushing them out of the danger zone. Once they were out of the main press of the crowd, the cyclos ran with them and then bodily inserted Cwiz and Trav back into the basket seats on the handlebars. They all cycled away to safety.

Laughing nervously as they sped away, Trav found that his camera had been ripped out of his pocket. Cwiz inspected himself and found only a few scratches.

Back at the hotel that night, Cwiz reflected on what felt like a near-death experience. He felt lucky to have escaped without a scratch and thought he might have pushed it a bit too far this time. Trav sarcastically mused that perhaps throwing other human beings was a bad idea.

Before bed, Cwiz pulled out two Christmas ornaments he had purchased at the market earlier in the day, and he carefully packed them up with paper he scrounged from around the room. Then he wrapped them in a sweatshirt and placed them in the middle of his pack, figuring they would be safest there. When he returned home weeks later, he pulled out the ornaments and put them in the plastic storage bin with the letter and figurines hidden in the back of his closet.

Life Lesson:
Make friends with some locals when you get into town; it could save your life.

CHAPTER 39

THE STANK IN HERE IS UNREAL

Cwiz was in a dark underground corridor in Rome, on yet another trip to Europe, his fourth. Cwiz, Bill, another high school leader named Steve, and five high school students were making their way to the subway to get to the Colosseum. When the train arrived, they saw it was absolutely crammed with tourists.

They piled into the train car, shoving people to make room for the eight of them. Once inside, Cwiz grabbed an overhead handle to balance himself. A very large, sweaty man was holding a strap directly next to him. The man's armpit was six inches from Cwiz's face.

Cwiz yelled across the car to Bill, who was now twenty feet away and behind forty other passengers.

"Hey, Bill, do you smell that?"

Cwiz leaned into the dude's armpit as he said it.

Bill looked down and tried to ignore him, pretending Cwiz must be talking to someone else.

"Bill, seriously, bro, do you smell what's happening in here? Hey, Bill, with the blue LA Dodgers hat on and the white shirt. Bill, do you smell that?!"

Steve and the other dudes were dying, hunched over and convulsing. Bill continued to look in the other direction, pretending to be oblivious. He would not be broken.

"Bill, the stank in here is unreal! And it starts with this guy right here." Cwiz pointed to the large man whose armpit was directly on top of him.

The large man, apparently perfectly fluent in English, sheepishly lowered his arm and used his other arm to hold on to a different strap.

The students were practically wetting themselves laughing. The trip was going well.

About three months earlier, Cwiz had been sitting at P.F. Chang's with five of his high school student mentees from the church youth group, talking about their futures. They were scarfing down plate after plate of pan-fried pork dumplings as they discussed the possibilities.

This group of Cwiz's dudes was about to graduate from high school, meaning they had been the beneficiaries of Cwiz's antics and methodologies for the past four years in the church youth group. The five students were Jake, Josh, Sean, Kyle, and Gordo. The guys were talking about what they were going to do after graduation. They talked about jobs, going to college, the usual pathway. Cwiz, never having pursued that path, listened to them explain these common stresses, wondering why they were all going the same direction when they were all so different.

Cwiz scratched his head, knowing he was a real-life example of a dude who was financially successful by any standard, was well-informed (by simply reading the paper and *Newsweek* and *Time Magazine*), and yet, he had no plaque on a wall from a university declaring that he was educated. He also wondered why none of them were taking this opportunity to go see the world.

He said, "Guys, listen to me. There is more to life than choosing the right college. For some of you, you need to see the world, and let that be your education."

Kyle said, "It would be so cool if we could all travel somewhere."

Cwiz smiled and popped another dumpling into his mouth. "Why can't we?

The guys all looked stupidly at each other.

Cwiz said, "Okay, here's what we'll do. We'll go to Europe for your spring break this year."

The dudes were immediately amped on this idea and said they were all on board. But they all agreed it would be tough to get their families to allow them to go.

Cwiz said, "Leave that to me."

Cwiz told the high school pastor Bill about the idea that day. Bill thought it was nuts, and that there was no way these parents were going to let Cwiz take their kids to Europe. Bill thought the parents would immediately shut down this crazy idea.

But Cwiz had a plan. He called a meeting of all the parents at his house and within a week, the five sets of parents sat in his living room. Cwiz's roommate, Steve, also a high school leader, was invited to come along. Steve stood in the back of the room as Cwiz put on his presentation. Bill was also there to see this dog and pony show.

Cwiz told the parents he was a seasoned traveler (which was true), had been everywhere (which was mostly true), and had specifically been exactly where they were going, Spain (also true). He told them that with three leaders (Cwiz, Bill, and Steve), and only five students, they would be able to keep good tabs on the boys. He told them the cost would be only $500 per student, and he would take care of the rest.

In other words, Cwiz was going well into his pocket to take care of the airfare, hotels, and food for their time in Europe with a group of eight. The parents were more than satisfied, and it was on.

Cwiz kept the trip entirely under wraps. All he told the group, including Steve and Bill, was that they were flying to Madrid on Day 1. The rest of the trip was completely a secret, and Cwiz planned it all out on his own.

The day arrived, and with a high level of excitement, the eight of them hopped on a flight to Spain. Apart from Cwiz, none of them had been to Europe before. In fact, most of them had barely left home.

After tooling around Madrid, Cwiz told them they were all heading back to the airport and whisked them away to Paris on a late-night flight. When they got to Paris, they found a hostel last minute and shacked up for the night. They spent two whirlwind days seeing everything they could in Paris.

Two days later, Cwiz again surprised them, this time with a flight to Rome, and the news was received with hearty cheers. When they got to Rome, however, it was pouring rain and the excitement was wearing off. After getting off the train, the group plodded through the rain, laden with gear and complaining like soldiers. When they had gotten close to their chosen hostel, they stopped in a restaurant to escape the downpour.

The restaurant was too nice for them—eight sweaty, stinking, drenched Americans. Cwiz, speaking English with a bad Italian accent from a Scorsese movie, ordered margherita pizzas for everyone. Then he took his shoes off and removed his soaking wet socks.

Cwiz's kryptonite is socks. He can't handle wet or dirty socks on account of some sensory sensitivity deep within his brain. When his socks get dirty, some synapse trips like a circuit and he shuts down until he takes care of it. For a time, Cwiz was buying socks in bulk and wearing a brand-new pair every day. Once worn, they were forever unclean and banished from the world.

So, with a look of disgust, he took off his wet socks and left them on the floor.

Bill scolded him. "What are you doing?"

"My socks are soaked. I can't wear these."

"Yeah, all of our socks are soaked, but you can't take them off in here."

"Why not?"

"Because it's gross and they stink, and people are trying to eat."

"They can't smell 'em. It's fine."

Steve said, "Dude, c'mon."

Bill threw up his hands and looked out the window at the rain. The rest of the guys were excited to be in a new city and talking about what they'd do tomorrow.

When they finished their pizzas, Cwiz put his shoes back on without the socks, leaving them under the table. The group had walked back out into the rain when they heard someone call out.

Behind them, the waiter ran toward them, shielding his head from the rain with a menu. The waiter said, "Eskoozy, this is yours." He held out a fist with two dripping wet tube socks to no one in particular in the group.

Cwiz said, "Gordo! C'mon, man. You can't leave your socks in there."

Gordo stepped forward, barely able to stand up because he was laughing so hard, and he took the socks from the waiter.

Because I was not there for this Europe trip, I called up Steve to chat him up about what he remembers from this trip with Cwiz. Steve is an insightful dude, and he has always seemed to be wise beyond his years. He now makes a living as a psychologist, doing exactly what he should be doing, helping people navigate life's ups and downs. Because he lived with Cwiz for about three years during this period of time, he has unique insight into the man.

Here's a snapshot of part of our conversation as I interviewed him for this chapter:

Me: Tell me about what you remember of the trip.

Steve: It was a complete blur. It was like five countries in eight days. The whole thing was crazy because nobody even knew where we were going. Cwiz had this whole trip planned out, but he was the only one who knew what city was next. He just blew these kids' minds, one day after another, one sight after another.

Me: What was he trying to do?

Steve: I think he wanted to open their eyes to the world. We were hitting up these historical sites every day, and he was actually trying to teach them some history, I think. Then again, we were acting like complete idiots at the Louvre.

But I think his goal overall was to light a spark in them, to grab the bull by the horns, I guess.

Me: The bull being what?

Steve: (Pause) It's sort of hard to put into words, but that quote from Howard Thurman comes to mind. He said, "Ask yourself what makes you come alive and go do that, because what the world needs is people who have come alive." I think what Cwiz really wanted was to help these guys come alive.

LIFE LESSON:
Find your passion and come alive.

CHAPTER 40

GRACE'S SON

Cwiz had settled into life as a car salesman for several years. He was making what he thought was pretty decent money—not huge money, but good money for a dude just out of high school with no college education. But he found the hours long and many quiet nights at the dealership boring. On rainy nights sometimes, the car lot looked like a ghost town and there was not a single customer to talk to. He got restless and resented the fact that he sometimes had to sit there at work for no reason, wasting time.

He found that he could sell cars at any dealership, *i.e.*, he could sell any type of car, and he also found that he could move around from place to place without any trouble at all. Car dealerships were always hungry for new salesmen, especially those with a wheelbarrow full of "Salesman of the Month" plaques.

So Cwiz fell into a pattern where he would sell cars for several months, rack up the awards, save up some money, and then quit. He would then venture off into the world, traveling until he ran out of money. Returning home, he would then present himself in suit and tie at a new dealership, get hired, and become the best salesman again. Then he would quit again and travel.

Cwiz went everywhere on his furloughs from work. He traveled through South America for a time with Cory, venturing into the jungle and sleeping in huts, hanging from a rickety and wet railing over a massive waterfall called Iguacu Falls, playing dominoes in huts with locals as the rain fell in heavy sheets. While traveling in South America, he met a dude named John Duffy, an Australian, and after Cory went home, Cwiz continued on with Duffy through Argentina. He visited his mother's family there and rode horses on a family ranch like a gaucho. Later he visited Duffy in Australia and toured the sights. Duffy, a sailor, let Cwiz take the wheel of a sixty-foot sailboat as they skated over the water in Sydney Harbor.

After his trip to Argentina and Australia, Cwiz unpacked an Argentine soccer jersey that he had purchased in Buenos Aires. He folded it up as neatly as he could and pulled out the plastic storage bin from the back of his closet. The bin now contained several letters, figurines, and Christmas ornaments. He laid the jersey on top. Then he put the storage bin back in its place.

Cwiz's mom, Graciela, watched his disjointed lifestyle closely, the way he nomadically roamed the earth, never settling down. When they were still living together at their home in Fountain Valley, she approached him with an idea. Being a real estate agent herself, she knew Cwiz could sell homes if he could sell cars. And she knew he would be an exceptionally successful agent, given his people skills. She told him so one day, explaining to him that as a real estate agent, he would not have to quit his job every time the travel bug bit him. He could simply get his agent's license, travel when he wanted to, and make his own schedule. He could also make more money, while spending less time working.

Once the seed was planted, it would not be dislodged. The idea made perfect sense to him, so as he continued to sell cars, and while he prepared to go on another trip, he started studying for the real estate exam.

In 1999, he passed the exam and started selling homes, taking a job as an agent at a local agency where Graciela used to work. Cwiz's client list immediately skyrocketed. Everyone knew Cwiz, and it took very little effort to get his name out there. We joked that he was the unofficial mayor of Fountain Valley. In the first year as a real estate agent, he doubled his salary, even while he found time to travel.

Immediately after making some money in real estate, Cwiz started thinking of ways to make this newfound success fun for everyone. He wanted to share it with his friends. His solution was to throw a massive party for just about every single person he had ever met in his life. In his second year as an agent, he threw a party, ostensibly to thank his clients for their support. He invited hundreds of people and rented out a huge ballroom. He invited buddies from high school, his extended family members, all his buddies' parents, old ladies at church he barely knew, and old acquaintances from far and wide. He arranged for random giveaways, karaoke, casino games and raffles, food and drink. It was an absolutely huge and successful party, and one that people were talking about for a long time, which is to be expected when you walk out of a party with a new Cuisinart.

His real estate business continued to increase as a result of his phenomenal networking skills, but because he was working as an agent under the supervision of another broker, he was giving a portion of all of his commissions to the broker. In true Cwiz fashion, he thought to himself, *Why would I want to do that*?

So he sat for his broker's exam, passed, and obtained his broker's license. As a broker, he was permitted to supervise other agents. Because agents need a supervising broker, agents pay commissions to the broker. Cwiz decided to pay more commission than other brokers, and in no time, he signed up close to fifty agents. Wisely, he hired Amanda, a gal he knew from junior high, to be his right-hand person and keep the train on the track on a daily basis. Before he knew it, he was making more money than he had ever made in his life.

When he needed a name for his brokerage, he asked all of his clients (and pretty much everyone he knew) to submit possible names for his company. He told everyone that whoever submitted the best name would win an all-expense-paid trip to Maui for a week. He picked a winner submitted by a dude named Ricky P. and named the company Grason Homes. The name "Grason" had meaning. It meant "Grace's Son." Ricky P. scored a nice week in Maui as a result.

And as he sold one home after another, Cwiz was struck by how often people asked him for a referral to a reputable contractor to handle the remodeling they wanted to do on their new homes. Seeing another opportunity, Cwiz studied for his general contractor's license, passed it, and another company was born: Grason Construction.

LIFE LESSON:
Listen to your mother.

PART FOUR

THIRTYSOMETHING

Cwiz (left), the legendary wedding dancer, with me and Bri gettin' funky in the background.

Chapter 41

Calico Jones

"**M**r. Chung Mao Bank Manager of Bank of China, Taiwan Branch, China" had an "urgent" and "very confidential" business proposition for Cwiz. It was so important that Mr. Chung Mao Bank Manager of Bank of China, Taiwan Branch, China sent the confidential message to Cwiz via email.

The urgent confidential proposition was this: Mr. Mao's bank had received a $30 million deposit from a man named Lawrence Smith, and the bank was trying to send the money back to Mr. Smith because his deposit period had ended, but Mr. Smith apparently had croaked, with no "WILL" and with no next of kin. To make matters worse, Mr. Mao explained, according to the laws of China, the money would revert to the government if no one claimed it.

Oh no!

Well, lucky for Cwiz, Mr. Mao's elegant solution for this conundrum was that Mr. Mao "will like you as a foreigner to stand in as the next of kin to Mr. Lawrence Smith so that the fruits of this old man's labor will not get into the hands of some corrupt government officials."

What a great idea, Mr. Mao!

Mao suggested that Cwiz simply send his name and address so that the attorney could draw up the paperwork (read: the fake will). Then Cwiz needed only to provide his bank account information, and the $30 million would be transferred to him. Mao reasonably suggested that they split the money 90/10, with 27 million going to Cwiz, and 3 million going to Chung Mao.

If Cwiz felt any trepidation at all about this transaction, Chung Mao reassured him that "there is no risk at all as all the paperwork for this transaction with be done by the attorney and my position as the Bank manager guarantees the successful execution of this transaction."

Phew.

Now, I'm guessing most of you have at some point in your lives received an email along these lines. Perhaps it was from a Nigerian prince or other such royalty purportedly from some far-off part of the world. In every case, though, the sender promises a huge sum of money if you will only provide some private details so that they can deposit the money into your bank account. I'm also guessing that after you got about three lines into the email (probably not even that far), you deleted it and carried on living your life.

That, right there, is why Cwiz is a different sort of animal than you. While you were annoyed that your inbox had been defiled by a filthy scam artist, Cwiz saw nothing but an incredible opportunity. Cwiz read the email with interest from beginning to end and composed a response.

This was Cwiz's response to Chung Mao's email:

Dear Mr. Chung Mao:

Yes, I am very interested. How do we proceed?

Calico Jones

This brief reply no doubt excited Mr. Mao. He must have turned around to his bank of scam artists at the internet café and said, "Yes! I've got a live one here."

What followed was an epic saga of push and pull between two scammers, each intent on screwing with the other. There were many, many emails. Mao tried every trick to get Cwiz to give him the information he needed, and Cwiz kept distracting him with non-sequitur demands.

Cwiz eventually wore Mao out. Perhaps it was Cwiz's constant demands that they use code names, and that Mao use a different code name every single time he composed an email. Perhaps it was Cwiz's repeated questions about Mao's toes: *How many toes do you have? What are they like?* Perhaps it was Cwiz's delving into family problems he was having, and Cwiz's suggestion that his Uncle Chip may have murdered his cousin. Perhaps it was Cwiz's repeated reference to a mysterious relative code-named "the Hairy Jackal" who was going to come with him (*i.e.*, with Calico Jones) to Amsterdam to collect the millions. Or it may have been Cwiz's demand that Mao send him a photo of his family. In any event, eventually Mao gave up, saying he was confused by all the questions.

The email correspondence between these two is lengthy and hilarious. I could not possibly summarize it all here, but I'll give you a taste. Here's an email from Cwiz to Mr. Mao, well into their email relationship:

Dear Partner:

I just want you to know that you are not acting like a partner right now! I am a little mad at you because I already told you that I am willing and able to travel whenever you need me to. I can leave tomorrow, with all my Toes!!! You just have to tell me where to go. I will say one thing—I am very cautious now because you have not told me very much about you.

I asked you to send me a photo… YOU NEVER DID!!!

I asked you to give each of us a code name… YOU NEVER DID!!!

I am starting to think this is some kind of emotional game you are playing with my heart. Do you really want this to happen or not? Are you just trying to use me like my last wife Fernanda did? She married me then took the BMW and also the house we had on the most beautiful lake here (Lake Elsinore) and she left me with about $54,000 in shopping bills. So give me what I want "Partner" and start acting like a partner and not some snotty-nosed kid with his thumb up his HELLO OPERATOR. I will wait for your reply and I want you to know I will fly to Europe as soon as you tell me to. This is a lot of money we are about to share, stop acting like a clown!!

Remember I love you and want only what's best for you my little Chung Pie.

Peace on earth,

Soft Cloth

Soft Cloth was one of Calico Jones's ten code names in their email exchanges. I could not do justice to the entire exchange, but it is the most ridiculously silly correspondence imaginable.

But lucky for you, after the email correspondence ended with Mr. Chung Mao Bank Manager of Bank of China, Taiwan Branch, China, years ago, Cwiz published the entire exchange in a book called *The Adventures of Calico Jones*. Cwiz graciously granted me permission to include the emails in this book (see "Appendix: The Adventures of Calico Jones").

LIFE LESSON:
Never pass up an opportunity to scam a scammer.

CHAPTER 42

PROM TRIP

Cwiz was fiercely devoted to the students he mentored at church. Every four years or so, he was handed a new set of five or six high school students. They were his to mold, his little experiments. He knew what it was to be a sort of chubby spaz with bad hair in junior high, and what it was like to be a hyperactive high schooler, hopped up on pheromones without knowing what to do with them. Cwiz worked on convincing his students that being a weirdo was good, and that having ridiculously silly times was not only good, but imperative in life.

One night while working with his small group of dudes, the subject of prom came up. It was the usual discussion about who they should ask, what kind of outfit they were supposed to wear, and what kind of transportation they should arrange. Much of the conversation was centered on how they were going to pay for all this. A tuxedo would set a kid back $100, the prom tickets would cost another $100, and if you're asking someone to go with you, double that. Then there were transportation costs, dinner, etc.

Cwiz said, "Okay, look, guys. You gotta do this right, because you only really get to do this once. So I have a proposal for you: I'll pay for everything, but I have one condition."

The guys were excited, and they all leaned in.

Cwiz continued, "The condition is this: You wear what I say. I pick the outfits you wear. But dinner, transportation, and the tickets are on me."

As one man, the group said, "Deal!"

A week later, Cwiz drove the guys to a costume shop and picked out the most ridiculous outfits he could find. One of the students dressed up as Napoleon, another was dressed as a Civil War general, and yet another was a member of a mariachi band with a massive sombrero.

Just before the night of the prom, Cwiz went to work to find a limousine to rent for the students and their dates, but all of them were rented out. He had waited too long to book it. So he looked for backup transportation and eventually settled on one of those giant red double-decker English-style buses. Of course, the massive bus would be a lot more expensive for Cwiz, but he decided it was worthwhile. He really wanted to give these kids a night to remember. Because he now had a huge vehicle that could hold sixty kids, Cwiz told them to invite all their friends.

On the night of prom, Cwiz had all the kids meet at a central location to board the bus. Sixty dolled-up students showed up and piled onto the bus. Over a hundred parents were there to shoot photographs of their soon-to-be-adults, wondering how they had all gotten so big. Cwiz stood in the back, full of pride, as the pictures were taken of his crew in their stupid costumes. The dudes and their dates were loving it, already having a fantastic time. Cwiz waved as they drove away, and told the parents he had a surprise planned for the kids.

Cwiz arranged for the bus to take the kids to dinner at a buffet in Long Beach, a thirty-minute drive away. The reason Long Beach was his choice for dinner was because Cwiz happened to have a friend who worked with the Long Beach Police Department. So, after they finished dinner, the students excitedly piled back onto the bus, ready to go to prom. But they were immediately pulled over by Long Beach's finest—Cwiz's cop buddy. Let's call him Al; I don't want to get him in trouble.

Al the cop sauntered slowly to the bus, and the bus driver, in on the joke, played along. Al stepped onto the bus and ordered all the kids to sit down. Thirty prom dresses folded into the plastic seats. He walked up and down the aisles until he found one of

Cwiz's students, Kyle, and dragged him off the bus, saying, "You. Come with me."

Kyle said, "What'd I do?"

"I saw you throwing beer bottles out of the bus."

The kids all started freaking out, telling the cop they weren't drinking, that no one threw anything.

"Are you calling me a liar?"

The kids had no response. Al pulled Kyle out onto the street and put him in the car.

Al got back on the bus. "I'll need statements from each of you. We're going to be here a while."

One of the girls said, "My parents are going to kill me."

Another girl pleaded, "We're going to miss prom."

Just then, Cwiz ran onto the bus. "You guys just got punked!"

The kids all screamed and yelled as a hot air balloon full of anxiety vanished in an instant. Then they headed off to prom with a police escort and a prom story they would never forget.

LIFE LESSON:
Dress up like an idiot once in a while.

CHAPTER 43

NANA SANDWICHES

Cwiz liked to get busy with people's nanas at weddings. He had been doing this on the dance floor at our friends' weddings for a long, long time. It started in the late '90s, when the engagements and weddings first started breaking out everywhere. Our group of friends was hitting our mid-twenties then, and all of us were getting married—all except Cwiz.

Because Cwiz was perennially single, there was a lot of talk about him in those days. *When will he find someone? Do you think he can calm down enough to hold down a relationship? Why can't he just be happy with her? I mean, she's a great girl?!*

Cwiz seemed to expertly avoid long-term relationships. He floated from one girl to the next, drifting easily into and out of brief relationships, never fully smitten and never pissing anyone off too badly when he moved on. As the only non-married dude in our group, he was the odd man out, but he appeared to be comfortable with the role.

It was as if he decided he would let us graduate from college, settle down, start having kids, and go the conventional route. While we did that, he would hold down crazy-town for us. He would stay single, fly to an Argentina World Cup game on a whim, and show up at our weddings and dance with our nanas. He would keep the stories going and have something hilarious for us when he showed up to have dinner with us and the kids. The kids would shout, "Uncle Giggles is here!" when he came in the door, and he would entertain them with his boundless energy. That was Cwiz's role not only for my family, but for all of our families. Cwiz's name was changing to Uncle Giggles, and that was what all our kids called him.

Wedding after wedding came and went. Cwiz donned a rented tuxedo time and time again. He was a groomsman a record-breaking number of times. Guys he barely knew would invite him to be part of the wedding because they knew he would bring the juicy giggles to their party.

At the wedding receptions, when the dance floor was crowded with ironic dance moves from the cool kids and terribly earnest dancing from the not-so-cool kids, when people were just starting to get a little loose, Cwizzy would make his move. He would surreptitiously tip the DJ a twenty and request "Livin' La Vida Loca" by Ricky Martin as the next song. (It was either that or something from Gipsy Kings.) Once the song started, it was his time.

He bulled his way through the crowd to the floor and cleared a circle for himself. He stomped in dramatic Flamenco style with his right leg on the wooden floor, he whirled and preened, and he yelled out the Spanish lyrics over the blare of the speakers. At some predetermined point in the song (he had this down to a science by now), he made his way out of the circle through the crowd to find a nana. The nana would be clapping absentmindedly to the song, wondering what in God's name was happening in the middle of that dance floor.

Cwiz would appear before her, hold out his hand, walk her to the dance floor, and encourage her to dance, which she would always do, so adorably. He would dance with her, gyrating ridiculously with her, and remind her of earlier days. She would love every second of it.

When he could manage it at a wedding, and if there were sufficient living relatives on both sides of the family, *i.e.*, if there were two nanas, then he would often get them both out there, and he would get a "nana sandwich" going, with him in the middle, and a nana dancing on either side of him. I am sorry to say that twerking was often involved, and that the nanas seemed to enjoy this most of all. The image of my wife's nana attempting to twerk is seared into my brain, like the charred scar from a branding iron.

Cwiz and our buddy Mark dancing with Bri's nana at our wedding.

And then there were the times when his chosen dance partner got out of hand. On one occasion, Cwiz was in particularly fine form. He stood on a table before hundreds of cheering wedding attendees, dancing and sweating through his rented shirt. With an air mic in hand, he lip-sync'd Ricky Martin's classic with a vein popping out of his forehead. The crowd was going bonkers. His eyes surveyed the room from the top of the table and fell on the mother of the bride, who was shaking her hips and laughing maniacally, martini in hand. Cwiz leapt off the table, spun with the grace of a matador, and made his way to her.

She smiled flirtatiously when she saw him coming for her. She placed her martini emphatically on the table and immediately accepted his invitation to dance, without a hint of hesitation. She really wanted to dance with Cwiz. Once she got on the floor, we saw one of her heels wobble. *Yep, she was wasted.*

Cwiz knew that he may have bitten off more than he could chew this time. She pressed herself close to him and wrapped her arms around him, squeezing him to her bosom. He kept dancing, smiling to the crowd, and trying not to meet the eyes of the bride's father, who had now taken a keen and frowning interest in this glorious spectacle.

When he finally tried to push away from her, she squeezed him harder and whispered into his ear, "My God, you're sexy!"

LIFE LESSON:

It wouldn't kill you to twerk with your nana once in a while.

CHAPTER 44

CENTRAL PARK DATE WITH STEVE-O

Cwiz and Steve, as roommates, went through what they described as the "dry years"—the long winters with no activity on the dating front. Because Steve was a college student at the time, Cwiz kept encouraging him to bring over some lady friends from school.

Steve finally invited a couple girls over to the house on Halloween. The girls had never met Cwiz, and he wanted to make his usual big impression. So he told Steve to tell them they were going to a park for a special Halloween scare. Cwiz then contacted a couple of his former high school students and told them he had a mission for them.

Cwiz called up Kyle, who had been on the whirlwind trip to Europe with Cwiz and Steve a few years before.

"Listen, Kyle. Steve-O and I are taking some girls out tonight and we want you to do something for us."

Kyle said, "Whatever you need, man."

Cwiz explained that he wanted Kyle to hide out at Central Park, and to get some other dudes to come with him if he could. They would bring the girls to the park, and he wanted them to jump out and scare them.

Kyle asked, "You think this will help?"

Cwiz said, "Yes, of course. Just do it."

They arranged to hide in a specific location, and Cwiz started planning out an excuse to get the girls to a dark and scary park on Halloween in the first place. Well, Cwiz and Steve-O succeeded in getting the girls to walk with them through the park. But Kyle was a little too good at his job, and when he started cracking twigs in the bushes behind them, and standing there stoically with his psychopath's mask, quietly brandishing a fake knife while barely visible in the shadows, the girls were terrified.

One of the girls started screaming like she was being stabbed by his play knife. They all started running, and she screamed nonstop. While Cwiz and Steve-O tried to calm her down and explain that the dude was their friend and they had set the whole thing up, Kyle snuck back to where Cwiz had parked his truck and hid under the truck.

Now the girls were in on the prank, but one of Kyle's buddies continued with the mission and jumped out at them. The girls started screaming again, and they all ran back to the parking lot. When they got within 100 yards of Cwiz's car, they saw through the trees that the lights of a police car were flashing next to theirs. Blue flashing lights and a spotlight from the cruiser fully illuminated Cwiz's car.

Then they saw Kyle handcuffed and sitting on a curb, trying to explain. The cop was yelling at Kyle to shut up.

Cwiz ran over and, in the words of Steve-O, got all "Papa Bear" to protect Kyle. Well, running up on a cop is not the best idea, and that did not go over well. Cwiz ended up arguing with the police officer, trying to explain that this was all a joke, that Kyle was not actually Leatherface in the flesh. The cop had to explain that all the screaming resulted in a number of calls about a possible rape in the park.

Several other cops arrived, and all of the guys got chewed out.

So, to sum up, there was no making out and they never saw the girls again.

After that miserable failure of a date, Cwiz took pen to paper and wrote a letter, once again to a person he had never met. When he was done, he took the letter, folded it, and put it in the plastic storage bin in the back of his closet, which was now nearly full.

LIFE LESSON:
People don't like to be scared.

CHAPTER 45

Game Show Lovin'

Cwiz's general approach to dating has been described, like a wartime campaign, as "Shock and Awe." On a first date, Cwiz would dream up something huge. He never seemed to just take a girl out for a cup of coffee. The first date had to blow her mind and all of her expectations. He wanted the girl to feel like it was the best date of her life, right out of the gate.

He had a go-to move of sorts on many of his first dates. He would buy flowers, but not to bring to his date's house. Instead, he would stop by a Wendy's or a Jack in the Box near her house and pull into the drive-through. He would ask the cashier to hold the flowers there for him and say that he would be back in fifteen minutes.

Then he would go pick up his date, and once they were on the way, he would tell her he wanted to stop at the drive-through for a snack. She'd inevitably point out that they were on their way to dinner. He'd say, "Yeah, but I'm thirsty."

She'd be confused, but then he'd pull up to place his order: "A Coke, easy ice, and some flowers, and I have a good neighbor discount." He'd drive around to the window and be handed a dozen roses. He would hand the roses to her: "This is for you."

Well, that usually worked in his favor to start the date. As he and his dates got older, and he had more disposable cash, the romantic gestures on the first dates became bolder. I am not going to run through all of the details here, but suffice to say, there were helicopters involved.

But he couldn't live up to these over-the-top gestures after the first date, and he (and she) would move on. He had not yet met the girl that would sustain his interest long term, and he would flame out after the first date.

So what does a guy do when he's in a dating rut?

You got it! He goes on a television game show—more specifically, a dating game show.

This particular show would pick a love-starved contestant who was then presented with three eligible mates to choose from for a date. The two went out on their date, but this all happened before the show was taped. After the date, the couple went on the show separately to discuss with the host how the date went.

Cwiz was the love-starved contestant, and he picked a girl he thought was cute out of a photo and video line-up. During the date, he arranged for them to be pulled over by a police officer who was a friend of his (the same guy—Al—who had pulled over the students on prom night).

Al leaned into the window and asked the girl, "Is this a date?"

She said, "Yes, Officer."

"Did he bring you flowers?"

She looked confused. "Uh…no."

Al said, "I'll be right back." He walked back to his cruiser and returned with a ticket, handed it to Cwiz and said, "Sign here. This is not an admission of guilt. It just says you have to pay me back for the flowers." Al then handed a bouquet of flowers to Cwiz's date through the window.

She accepted the flowers and melted into the seat. Afterward, however, they had a rather tedious dinner, at least from Cwiz's perspective, and he was bored the entire time. Cwiz hoped the flowers story would be on television, to at least boost his dating "cred" with the other eligible ladies in the world. But the producers did not want to tell that story.

Instead, after the date, the producers asked Cwiz about the date and if he wanted to go out with her again. He said no. They told him, "Well, let's tape the show and you guys can describe why it did not work out for you." Cwiz agreed to be on the show, and so did she. Easy enough.

But before the show was about to tape, the producers came to him in a sort of green room and told him excitedly that he better "have his guns loaded" because she was going to "tear him apart." Cwiz was dumbfounded. He thought they had gotten along fine, but if she thought she was going to embarrass him on television, he was going to make sure he got to her first. So he prepared to do battle for the cameras.

Cwiz found out later, from her, that the producers had come to her before the show and told her the exact same thing, that she better be ready to fend off an attack from Cwiz, because he was about to *tear her apart.*

The producers had totally set them up, making each of them defensive and hoping for fireworks on the show. And of course, it worked. When the TV host asked Cwiz on air what his first impressions were of the girl, Cwiz replied in one word, "Pasty."

The girl was aghast. It just went downhill from there.

Cwiz had hoped that the television show would raise his dating profile, but it was not to be. He was going back to the drawing board.

LIFE LESSON:
Communication is everything in a relationship.

CHAPTER 46

HERE COMES THE FUDGE

After more than a decade of watching all of his friends get married and have kids, there was some anxiety hanging around the edges of Cwiz's conscience. He figured it was probably time to make something happen on the relationship front. And there was talk at the church, quite a bit of talk, about when Cwiz was going to settle down (calm down, rather) and find someone. Cwiz was dating plenty, but no one stuck. Whenever I asked him about the latest girl who seemed great to me, he always had some vague complaint about her.

She walks funny.

Her ears are off center.

She likes cats too much.

But eventually, Cwiz started dating a girl we'll call Ann for the purposes of this story, who was a high school teacher. Ann was, to us, "solid," one he could potentially marry. There were a lot of people who were encouraging Cwiz to not let this one get away, to make this relationship stick.

But those of us who really knew him still wondered whether Ann was the right one, whether she was really up for his, shall we say, unique combination of personality traits. We knew it was going to take a certain special sort of person who would enjoy his antics but not get pushed around by his extremely forceful personality.

Being the good person that she was, Ann volunteered her time with the Make-A-Wish Foundation, and she had organized an event at Cold Stone Creamery, the ice cream shop, to raise money to make a kid's wishes come true. Cold Stone agreed to have "local celebrities" come to the ice cream shop and serve ice cream to patrons. The local celebrities were Cwiz, Bill (now the pastor at Cwiz's church), and another pastor named Dale.

When Cwiz, Bill, and Dale arrived at Cold Stone, Katelyn, a gal who worked there, started showing them how they serve up the ice cream in the unique Cold Stone way. They were taught to scoop the ice cream, slap it onto a freezing cold slab of stone, then mix in goodies of the customer's choice, be it Snickers, Oreos, fudge, peppermints, gummy bears, whatever, and then mash it up and put it into a cup or a cone.

Cwiz let her know that he had already worked in an ice cream shop for a brief time a decade ago and knew what he was doing. She was not impressed.

After they were briefly trained, the local "celebrities" started to get ready to serve the line of people forming outside the doors. Katelyn, satisfied that her trainees were ready, opened the door to the customers.

Given the successful promotion going on at the church, fifty people were lined up for the fundraiser and came right in the door. Cwiz was the first ice cream scooper behind the counter and he took the first order. It was for a hot fudge sundae. Cwiz picked up a squeeze bottle of fudge, held it high like Tom Cruise in *Cocktail*, and started drizzling fudge at elevation, a foot off the cold stone counter, down onto the ice cream.

The customer oohed and aahed as Cwiz spread the fudgey love so liberally. He held the fudge higher off the counter and did it again.

Another "OOOOHHH" emanated from the crowd.

The next person who ordered fudge got him a little more excited.

Cwiz yelled out, "Alllllriiiiiiighttt, everybody, we got some more fudge comin'!"

This time Cwiz grabbed two squeeze bottles of fudge, held one in each hand, and squeezed them from even higher, squirting them from head height onto the ice cream on the counter. The customers in line laughed and applauded as he played this up. He held up a handful of sprinkles and threw them into the air like Rip Taylor with confetti. It went all over the store. Katelyn frowned and went to find a broom.

Cwiz's girlfriend, Ann, who had organized this whole thing, was standing in the corner of the store and watching it all, in horror. She smiled weakly, trying to gauge whether Cwiz was going to ruin the entire night. At the next request for fudge from a new customer, Cwiz turned to Bill and said, "Bill, you might want to stand back for this."

Bill obediently took a step back.

After scooping out the ice cream and laying it on the slab, Cwiz again reached for the two squeeze bottles of fudge.

Cwiz yelled out in a deep voice, "Ladies and gentlemen! Here comes the fuuuuuuuuuuuuuudddddgggggggge!"

Cwiz held the bottles over his head and started spraying the fudge down on himself. He shouted as it rained down on his face and shook his head back and forth like a hungry shark.

He yelled out, "Now here comes the flashdance!"

Cwiz started dancing in place, shaking and writhing as he continued to squeeze out the fudge on his face and hot fudge flew around the room. Bill shot back to avoid getting splattered. Dale, oblivious to what was going on, kept working on his own ice cream and saying to himself, "Yeah baby, here comes the fudge."

The fudge was everywhere, and mixed as it was with Cwiz's face and hair, the store was now dealing with a health hazard.

Ann watched this insane display by her boyfriend with a now entirely blank smile on her face, utterly confused, probably wondering whether she should break up with him now or wait until the night was over. After the applause died down, Cwiz stood there awkwardly, cleaning himself up with a towel.

It got weirdly quiet, so he said with fudge smeared into his eyebrows, "Welp, I guess that's my time. See you later."

And he walked out.

Thankfully, the foundation did great that night and many wishes came true, especially for those who had never seen a grown man do a fudgey flashdance.

Ann and Cwiz broke up shortly thereafter and we all thought it was for the best.

LIFE LESSON:
If you can't take the fudge, get out of the kitchen.

Chapter 47

Montana

When I got divorced in 2005, I moved directly into Cwiz's house. Cwiz was roommates with Steve at the time, but they had an extra room and welcomed me in. My life was chaotic, to say the least. I was navigating the parameters of a new life on my own, making solo time work with my daughter, and trying to manage my typical heavy caseload at work.

While I struggled to get back on my feet, my law firm duties did not abate. The firm was not interested in relieving me of my caseload merely because I had personal problems, and in fact, almost no one at the firm even knew what was going on with me. So the firm was still counting on me to litigate my cases and get them ready for trial, as usual.

Just a few days after I moved in with Cwiz, I was designated to take a plaintiff's deposition the following Monday in Missoula, Montana. I did not know until Thursday that I would have to go, and I only had a few days to organize the trip and prepare for the deposition.

I realized immediately that this was a good opportunity to clear my head a little bit with some new scenery, if only for a few days. I could go to Montana early, on Friday, spend the weekend, and take the deposition on Monday.

I had never been there and was excited about the opportunity to look around, hike, and explore. But I knew that in my fragile state, I should not go alone. I needed to be around my buddies.

Not expecting them to actually go, I asked Cwiz and Cameron if they could drop everything and fly to Montana with me the following day. Because they are both unbelievably good friends, they both said yes. And just like that, the three of us were off on an adventure to Montana with virtually no plans for the weekend.

We arrived in Missoula on a beautiful late-August day. We tooled around town that night and decided to take a drive up to Kalispell the next day to hike at Glacier National Park.

We had a long drive through unusually beautiful countryside. Cam and Cwiz argued almost the entire drive about whether Angelina Jolie was actually a genuine philanthropist. Cam argued her alleged philanthropic acts were motivated purely by self-interest, and Cwiz argued she had a big heart and did it purely out of love for others. Because they were legitimately pissed at each other during the argument, which went on for over an hour, I thoroughly enjoyed myself, and wondered privately what the argument was really about.

We arrived in Kalispell and settled into a room in a chain hotel. We quickly went out to see what was going on in this small town. To give you an idea of the town, there are only about 20,000 or so people living there. It is a gateway town to the national park, and there is a backpacker vibe to the place.

We three dudes from Orange County, California, a county with 3 million people in it, were from a different world, and we felt completely out of place. That did not stop us, however, from going to the county fair, which just happened to be taking place the weekend we dropped in. We saw a stream of folks on the main drag, all walking and driving to the same place. We decided to see what was going on and found ourselves driving along with the others into a large dirt parking lot.

We walked up to the ticket seller, just outside a temporary chain-link fence that had been strung up to set up barriers for the fairgrounds. Inside the grounds, we could see rickety carnival rides that had no doubt been trucked in on flatbeds and erected by high-school dropouts just hours before. These rides looked sketchy as hell. I recognized one of the rides, the Zipper, as a popular one from the Orange County Fair back home.

Cwiz strolled right up to the guy manning the gate and taking tickets. The guy, I'm sorry to say, had literally one tooth on the top of his mouth. It was too much. The hillbilly carnie stereotype fit a little too snug on this guy.

Cwiz said, "Hey, buddy, how are you doin'?"

Toothless smiled. "I can't complain."

"Well, listen, my uncle is the assistant manager of the Zipper here."

Toothless leaned in to pay attention to this important news and mirrored Cwiz's earnest demeanor.

Cwiz continued, "So he asked us to come by and take a look."

"Uh-huh."

"He has to take off, but he wanted us to come by and make sure we had a smooth operation tonight for the Zipper."

"Uh-huh."

"So, we don't have any tickets, but we're just gonna pop in real quick and check, okay?"

"Oh, sure thing. You fellas have a good time."

So into the fair we went for free, to check on Cwiz's uncle's carnival ride. Once we got in, we marveled at the place. There were a lot of boots and hats. We wandered into an actual rodeo and watched genuine bulls with their nuts tied down throw real cowboys into the air. We shot pellet guns at targets to see who was the best. (It was Cwiz.) We rode a mechanical bull to see who could last the longest. (It was me.) And we did check out, but did not ride, the Zipper.

After the fair, we drove off to find something to eat—and a drink or four for me. We ended up in a sort of honky-tonk sports bar, and it being Saturday night, the place was fairly crowded. When we walked in, the folks in there all stopped what they were doing to take notice of us. It was not quite the cliché record-scratching moment you see in the movies, where the music stops and everyone stops talking and stares at the strangers coming into the bar, but it was pretty damn close.

With all eyes on us, we grabbed an open high-top in the middle of the bar. The waitress came over in about two seconds. With a flirty smile, she looked us over.

"How are you boys doin'?"

I said, "We're doing very well, thank you."

"And where are you all from?"

"Southern California."

"What brings you to Kalispell?"

"Divorce."

"Huh?"

"I'm getting divorced and needed a getaway, you might say, and these guys here are the two best friends a guy could have, so they joined me."

"Why Kalispell?"

"I had a little work to do in Missoula this week, and we decided to look around a little bit."

She smiled. "Glad you did."

She took our drink orders. I ordered an Old Fashioned, Cam asked for a Cadillac margarita (which I found endlessly entertaining, given the atmosphere), and Cwiz ordered a "Coke, easy ice," and then she was off to grab our drinks. Within seconds, the waitress had apparently downloaded what she knew to everyone in that bar.

In less than a minute, a gaggle of local girls moseyed over to our table and started chatting us up. And in less than five minutes, I was on to my second Old Fashioned and enjoying my discussion with my new friends. Cam and Cwiz were aloof.

Even as the whiskey began to do its work, I could tell the mood in the bar had somehow altered. I noticed more than a few squinted, unfriendly eyes underneath the large-brimmed hats around the room. A few of the cowboys in the place were apparently not too enthused about three dudes from Orange County arriving in their local bar and chatting up the local womenfolk.

The girls were loud, and one of them was a serious over-sharer. She told us about the dudes in the bar who were glaring at us.

"Oh, him, that jerk. He's my ex-husband."

"Seriously?" I said. "You were married to that guy?"

"Yeah, but he did not deserve me or our kids."

"How many kids do you have?"

"We have five."

"Holy...."

"Yeah, and he should be with them right now—horse's ass." She looked at him directly when she said it and emphasized the last two words. Then she elevated her voice and yelled across the room so he could hear: "HE KNOWS THIS IS MY NIGHT TO BE HERE!"

I said quietly, "Well, do you have to hang out in the same bar as your ex?"

"Where else am I gonna go?"

She had a point. As we talked further with the five women standing around our high-top table, we learned that we three dudes from OC were the only ones in the bar that they did not know intimately. Their exes, brothers, cousins, sisters, aunts, school-mates, and baby-daddies were all there drinking with them. We three were invaders.

Eventually, one of the dudes walked over congenially to our table. He was a large, corn-fed lineman of a dude, wearing a large belt buckle but no hat. He walked right up to us, all smiles but perhaps a little tipsy. He sidled up to Cwiz and stuck out his hand.

"Hey, guys. Name's Tim."

We all made "hi" and "how ya doin'" noises.

Tim continued, "I hear you boys are Californians."

Cwiz nodded. "But we love it here. Really beautiful place you have."

One of the girls piped up. "Tim, we were having a nice, friendly conversation...."

Tim cut her off. "I know, Jenny, I just wanted to meet these guys for myself."

Tim turned back to Cwiz, this time speaking only to him. "I have been wanting to visit California for a long time."

Cwiz said, "What part?"

"Well, that's the thing. I really don't know. I could use some advice, because I think I'll have a week or so to look around, but I need some pointers."

Cwiz said, "It's a big place. When are you going?"

Tim said, "You mind if we talk about this outside where I can hear you? I'll buy you a drink."

Cwiz looked at us, thinking nothing was amiss, and shrugged. "Sure thing, but no drink necessary."

Cwiz started walking out to the patio area with Tim, and Cam and I settled back into the conversation with Jenny and her friends. As soon as Cwiz got outside, I saw a commotion on the patio in my periphery. I turned to the right and saw Tim engaged in a full right-handed haymaker at Cwiz's face.

Cwiz threw his head backward to avoid the blow, and Tim's honeybaked ham of a fist grazed Cwiz's cheek. The momentum of his own punch threw Tim off balance, and his right arm went toward the ground. Cwiz, instinctively sensing the opportunity, shoved Tim forward and he went flying onto the ground, knocking over a patio chair and upending a table.

Cam and I were in shock, watching this scene unfold. We jumped up from our chairs, and Jenny grabbed us.

With saucer-sized eyes and a screech of fear, she yelled in our faces, "You boys gotta get outta here RIGHT NOW!!!"

Cam and I looked at each other and then looked around the room and saw the outside tables of cowboys start to assemble themselves for a butt-kicking. Cwiz ran back into the bar like a stampeding bull.

Jenny yelled again and started pushing us toward the door. "I said RIGHT NOW!!! The sheriff is coming, and he don't like outsiders!"

With Cwiz right on our heels, Cam and I ran for the front door and across the dirt parking lot to our car. As we jumped into the car, the doors of the bar flung open and Tim and six other ranch hands came running out.

Cam stomped on the gas as Cwiz fell into the back seat and we bumped and fishtailed out of the parking lot, leaving only a choking cloud of meandering dust in the moonlight.

Best. Night. Ever.

I frequently think about that night when it comes to Cwiz and his antics. The first thing I think about is the absolute terror in Jenny's face and her grabbing Cam and me the way she did and screaming her warning. I figure she has seen a few out-of-towners get their hides tanned in that bar for talking up the lady-folk. I guess there is a reason why scenes like that are cliché in movies, because such things actually happen all the time.

But the second thing that kills me is this: That night, Cwiz was not pushing the boundaries or seeing how much he could get away with. He was not annoying anyone, dumping toilet paper on anyone's head, or inconveniencing a stranger. He was simply trying to help a friendly dude named Tim have a nice visit to California, doing so with the best of intentions, and being a genuinely nice person. For that, Tim tried to cave in his face.

All the times he deserved to get punched, nothing happened, and the one time he deserved nothing but a free drink or a hearty thank you, he had to run for his life.

LIFE LESSON:
Never accept an invitation to talk outside with a cowboy.

CHAPTER 48

SNAKEBIT

Cwiz was writhing in pain in the passenger's seat of the van. Bill wore an expression of grim determination as he sped through the streets of a small Mexican town. Steve sat in the back, gripping the headrest of the seat in front of him, trying to see the road unfold in front of him.

Cwiz could feel his left hand beginning to stiffen. Two tiny punctures, an inch apart, were the only evidence of his wound. Through the fog of the pain, a thought came screaming into the forefront of his mind.

After everything I've done, is this really how I am going to die?

Cwiz had been with the church high school group in Mexico, building a house for the homeless. Before heading to the construction site, somebody discovered a small rattlesnake outside. Cwiz decided he had an opportunity to once again prove his fearlessness and all-around badassery to the group by picking up the snake and removing it from the area. He thought he could have some fun with it, maybe show off a little bit. But, of course, "There is no way to catch a snake that is as safe as not catching him."[1]

As he had done many times before, because it was something his dad made sure he knew how to do when he was young, Cwiz found a long stick and approached the snake. With a number of the students from the high school group and other leaders watching, he approached it carefully. He could see it was very small and probably very young, which made it more dangerous. They say young snakes release more venom when they bite than

---

1. This quote has been attributed to author Jacob Braude.

older snakes do, and a bite from this little guy was more likely to be fatal.

The snake perked up as he approached, and started rattling, warning Cwiz to stay back. Cwiz jammed the stick down on the snake's head, smashing it into the dirt so it could not move. Its body writhed violently as it unsuccessfully tried to escape. Cwiz then seized it by grabbing it right behind the head, squeezed hard, and picked it up. The snake's tail wrapped around his arm in a vain effort to apply some pressure to escape.

Cwiz held it up and showed it to the group, its beady eyes and closed mouth, protruding from Cwiz's clenched fist. "Now the serpent was more crafty than any of the wild animals the Lord God had made,"[2] and as Cwiz showed off the snake, he must have relaxed his grip just enough, because the serpent suddenly spun its head around in his hand and bit him right in the webby crease between his thumb and forefinger. As it bit down, it released a torrent of lethal venom into Cwiz, and its lifeless snake eyes seemed to glower at him with vengeful reproach.

Cwiz immediately threw the snake into the bushes. He then looked in horror at his hand, which was searing with red-hot fury. He could feel a curious searching sensation within his hand, as the venom began paralyzing his flesh and seeking its way to his heart.

Bill and Steve immediately hustled him into a van and started looking for a medic. The first place they found was a women's health clinic, but they ran in to talk to a doctor anyway. The doctor's face, after inspecting the wound, said all they needed to know. Steve, knowing not a word of Spanish, knew what this doctor was saying, because fear was written all over his face. He was saying to Cwiz, "You need to get yourself to a hospital equipped with anti-venom, as fast as you can."

This is bad, real bad, Steve thought.

---

2. Genesis 3:1.

They decided their best shot was to get to the US, and with the clock ticking, they sped to the border as fast as they could. Bill told me he remembers thinking two things while they were driving back to California: (1) how funny it was that Cwiz was going to die by snakebite; but (2) how horrible it was that Cwiz was going to die by snakebite—possibly at any moment.

When they got to the border, the line to exit the country seemed miles long. It would take far too long to get to the front. Bill said, "You guys get out here and run for it. Get a cab to the hospital. I will find you."

Steve and Cwiz jumped out of the car and started running to the border patrol station. Cwiz could hardly walk, much less run, he was in so much pain.

Steve flung open the door to the border station and told the station agent that they needed to get through immediately, that Cwiz had been bitten, and they needed to get to a hospital. The officer checked their ID's and then called an ambulance.

An ambulance was there quickly, and they were on their way. Steve jumped in the back with Cwiz in the stretcher.

While the EMT was checking Cwiz's vitals, Cwiz asked, "Am I going to be okay?"

The EMT said nothing, pretending not to hear the question.

Cwiz looked at Steve, terrified.

Steve asked the EMT again for him, "How does it look?"

The EMT shook his head and again said nothing at all.

Steve and Cwiz looked at each other, panic rising in each of them.

Steve tried to comfort him. "You're gonna be fine, dude."

When they arrived at a medical center in Chula Vista, Cwiz was immediately rolled into the ER. They began pumping him with anti-venom. One of the doctors took a black marker and put a hashmark on Cwiz's wrist, where the swelling was visibly creeping up his arm, and noted the time next to the hashmark. An hour later, another hashmark was applied to his mid-forearm.

After another few hours, the swelling was up to his elbow. Then another black mark was applied to show the progress of the deadly venom. The doctor explained that if the venom reached his heart, he could die and there would be nothing they could do. They just had to hope the anti-venom could get to work in time.

Steve and Bill sat helplessly in the waiting room. It was April 2, 2005, the day Pope John Paul II died, and they watched CNN while the ashes wafted from the Sistine Chapel. Steve felt it was an eerie omen. He had never seen Cwiz scared of anything, ever, and Cwiz's hopeless, fearful, far-off stare left him with a knot in his stomach.

On the first night in the hospital, Cwiz woke up alone. He thought, *This cannot be it for me.* He pondered the million crazy things he had done in his life and could not believe it had all led him to this ridiculously stupid ending. He thought about the letter he had written in Turkey that day while he sat alone in the town square, with his foot bleeding through the bandage. He could not accept the fact that he would never be able to deliver that letter.

He wanted to have a family, to fall in love, to raise children, to teach them how to live life to the fullest. He made a decision and a promise to God with a tear rolling down his cheek. *If I get out of here, I am going to settle down and stop acting like a clown. I am going to use my gifts to make the world a better place. With all the amazing experiences I have had, I am going to do all I can to create memorable experiences for others.*

Cwiz was ready to shed his skin, to slough into a new version of himself.

He lay there in the ICU for several days, cursing his foolishness. I called him from New Orleans, where I was on a business trip.

I said, "Bro, what the hell?"

Cwiz said, "I know."

"I heard what happened. What were you thinking?"

"Just doing my thing."

"Well, maybe it's time to do something else."

"You're right. I think things are going to be different now."

"So you're not going to be the next Croc Hunter?"

Cwiz chuckled. "No, I'm gonna get out of here and take it easy for a while."

"Good call."

Dan showed up to spend some time with Cwiz in the hospital, too. As a pick-me-up, Dan brought Cwiz's absolute favorite thing in the world—a box of Girl Scout cookies. Dan placed the small green box of goodness on the little hospital table next to Cwiz as he lay in bed sleeping. When Cwiz woke up and saw Dan, and then the Thin Mints, he managed to smile. Dan opened the box for him and held it out. Cwiz extended his giant, swollen hand, but it would not fit in the box.

Dan let him suffer a little. "What's the matter? Can't get any?"

They both laughed as Cwiz tried to stuff his swollen bear paw into the tiny box hole for a mint cookie.

Once Cwiz was home, the Captain's dad, Douglas, showed up, sat with him on the couch, and lectured him sternly in his Scottish accent. He said, "You'd sure look a proper fool dying like that, you know?"

Cwiz nodded, completely agreeing. "You're right."

Douglas asked, "Is it time to find a wife and raise some kids, do you think?"

"I think so."

LIFE LESSON:

There will come a time to get your shit together.

PART FIVE

GETTING IT TOGETHER

Cwiz and Jenna, a perfect match.

CHAPTER 49

THE COMPLETE PACKAGE

Jenna was driving her VW Jetta with Cwiz in the passenger's seat. Cwiz's friends Carolyn and Gordo were in the back seat. They were on their way to an ice cream cookie sandwich shop in Westwood. It was the first time Cwiz and Jenna had met. Cwiz had been visiting friends he knew at Pepperdine University. Jenna, a freshman there, was friends with his friends. When he got into Jenna's car, Cwiz gave her a hard time for driving a Jetta.

"A blonde in a Jetta. Typical," he said.

Not the best start.

Then Cwiz took over Jenna's radio and started blasting hard-core rap through the speakers. He was about to impress everyone in the car with his lyrical prowess when Jenna jumped in ahead of him, metaphorically grabbing the mic from his hands. Jenna belted out the lyrics, rapping in her lowest register, acting tough, emphasizing all the right syllables, especially the colorful adjectives, and firing off the words in rapid fashion.

Cwiz turned to her, intrigued. Here was this blonde, green-eyed beauty, a good Christian girl from a private Christian school, driving and rapping like an absolute boss.

Cwiz said to her, "Wow. I did not see that coming."

Jenna smiled. "I grew up in the 909."

Cwiz replied, "'Nuff said."

Cwiz was interested. But Jenna had a boyfriend, and the timing was not right. In fact, it would not be right for several years. From Jenna's freshman year until her senior year, she dated the other guy. But once in a while, as her college years passed, Cwiz checked in with her to see what was going on.

He emailed her, "Still got a boyfriend?"

"Yep."

"Okay then."

Cwiz bided his time and saw her occasionally. One summer, Carolyn invited Jenna to a summer houseboat trip with the church college group. Cwiz was on these trips as a college leader, so he saw Jenna two summers in a row. They talked here and there, and on one occasion, they spent an hour on the houseboat talking about their families. Jenna started thinking there might be more to this guy than just goofing off, but the timing was still not right.

After the houseboat trip, Cwiz was more intrigued by her and found silly ways to keep in touch. As a real estate agent, Cwiz had ordered those advertisement pads of paper with his name and face on them. You know the things that are stuffed in your door nearly every day from random agents? Cwiz had those, too, except his notepads had a picture of him from when he was five years old, riding a pony (not unlike the picture on the sweatshirt Cwiz asked David Letterman to wear several years before). The notepads were hilarious, and therefore memorable. He mailed one of those to Jenna during her sophomore year, along with $20 for some silly bet they made during the houseboat trip.

After several years went by, in December of her senior year of college (in 2005), Jenna finally broke up with her boyfriend. Shortly thereafter, Jenna sent Cwiz an instant message out of the blue.

"Hey, how's it going?"

"Good. Did you break up with your boyfriend yet?"

"Actually, yeah, I did."

"Reaaaaaaaallllllly?"

"Yep."

Cwiz decided at that moment it was going to be a full court press. He was going to win her heart. What followed was ten months of creative, intentional, and hard-core pursuit, with a lot of care packages.

Jenna was heading home for winter break that December and had to get her wisdom teeth out. She had mentioned this offhandedly to Cwiz online. So, after her surgery, a get-well care package arrived suddenly at her house. She thought, *This is amazing. Who does that?*

From January to March of Jenna's senior year at Pepperdine, Cwiz drove up from Orange County to Malibu twice a week on average, which took him a couple hours each way. They went to dinner every time he came up.

Cwiz is quite a bit older, so she did not see him at first as a potential boyfriend or husband. But she was open to hanging out with him. They kept having fun, so she kept an open mind. She continued to notice how easy it was with him, that he was a fun hang.

One night after dinner, after several weeks of hanging out, they were standing by the car and Cwiz had a bunch of DVDs in his hands for some reason. As she was about to head in for the night, Cwiz leaned in for a kiss and dropped the pile of DVDs all over the ground.

Cwiz shouted, "Oh man, I blew it!"

Jenna laughed.

"Oh, God, now what! Son-of-a! That was terrible."

Jenna was dying as Cwiz purposefully made a much huger deal out of it than was necessary. He played it up like a Chris Farley character on SNL (*"I am such an idiot"*) and made her laugh even more. They ultimately had an awkward hug and she went inside.

Once inside, she told her roommates what happened with his interrupted kiss. Her roommate Lindsy pressed her on her feelings for Cwiz. Jenna said they were just friends, but Lindsy corrected her, explaining that a guy who goes in for a kiss like that was not just a friend, and told her she needed to be careful not to lead him on.

Jenna knew she was right, and because she was on the rebound from her prior long relationship, she was worried she was jumping into something too soon. She needed to graduate, get a job, and see what life held for her. She needed to take it slow, and this was moving too fast. Cwiz, on the other hand, fresh off his snakebite and looking to get his life in order, was interested in something much more serious.

Jenna called Cwiz up the following day and told him she thought they needed to stay friends. He told her to do what she needed to do, but he wanted to be more than that. If she was not interested, then that was up to her. She hung up the phone, saddened that it was over.

But five days later, Cwiz called and told her he missed her. He told her he would take her as a friend if that was all she wanted. She agreed, and they carried on as if nothing had happened. Before they knew it, they were hanging out all the time, going to dinner, and Cwiz kept sending care packages.

St. Patrick's Day rolled around. It was March of Jenna's senior year. Cwiz figured it was a good excuse to do something silly and send another care package. He went to CVS and bought every single green thing he could find in the store and threw it in a box and mailed it to her. Jenna found herself opening up a package full of green highlighters, green Post-its, green bags of mints, green stickers, green silly string, and green sunglasses. She was once again befuddled and mystified. She found the silliness of his constant extravagant and thoughtful gestures was softening her.

Throughout the rest of the semester, random packages kept showing up for her. If they had talked about a TV show, like *Lost!* on the phone one night, then a package would show up within a couple days, and a *Lost!* sweatshirt was inside. Jenna lived in that sweatshirt for the rest of the semester.

Then they started talking on the phone every night for an hour or two. Despite the ground rules, Jenna found herself falling for him.

When graduation weekend rolled around, Jenna's family all came to the ceremony and they decided to have a celebratory lunch. Jenna wanted him to be there. Cwiz was not feeling well, but he would not miss it, and he showed up for lunch with her family.

As Jenna sat there watching her family meet and mingle with Cwiz, she knew they had reached a turning point. *Why is this guy even here if we are just friends?* Technically, that is what they were. They had not even kissed yet, but here was Cwiz sitting with her dad, stepmom, mom, and stepdad, yucking it up. She smiled to herself, looking at him, knowing that he was way more than just a friend now.

A week later, after he cooked for her (coconut shrimp), they had their first kiss, and they were official. But immediately after they reached this important step, Jenna had to leave. She had taken a temporary job in Missouri that summer and would be gone for five weeks.

Cwiz took it in stride and did what he always did. He started sending more packages. This time, he called on everyone he knew to send her letters and packages. Cwiz approached me and all the guys to write her letters. *Tell her how great I am*, he said. And we did. Every day for five weeks, Jenna got multiple pieces of mail, many of them telling her what a catch he was.

One day while she was there at camp, she got a letter from Cwiz that had a single puzzle piece in it. She thought the puzzle piece looked like a homemade photograph cut into pieces, but it was not clear what the picture would show. Each day, another puzzle piece arrived in the mail. After several weeks, the picture finally came together. It was a poster-sized picture of Cwiz holding a sign that said, "I like you." She taped it up and put it on the wall.

LIFE LESSON:
Persistence is key.

CHAPTER 50

VIA CHICAGO

Now done with her summer job, Jenna stuffed five weeks of postcards, letters, packages, and Cwiz's puzzle pieces into her bag. She hopped on a plane from Branson to Los Angeles, but it had a connecting flight in Chicago. She had not flown much at all by that point in her life, and certainly not by herself. She told Cwiz on the phone before she left how she was a little worried about the whole thing, making her connection, finding the gate, and the stress of it all.

When she landed at O'Hare Airport in Chicago, she sauntered through the crowded terminal and made her way to a bank of monitors that listed departure gates. As she studied the monitors to find the gate for her connecting flight, a man sidled up next to her, shoulder to shoulder. She didn't look but kept staring at the monitors.

He said, "What gate are you looking for?"

She knew the voice and turned to him.

"Omigod, what are you doing here?"

She gave him a long hug.

"Just in the area," Cwiz said with a smirk.

"Are you here for work or something? Why the heck are you in Chicago?"

"Because you're in Chicago!"

"But I'm flying home!"

"Yeah, I know. I bought a seat next to you for the flight home."

"You flew out here, just so you can fly home with me?" She thought she might cry.

He said, "Well, yeah, unless you want to stay here for a night, and see the sights."

"What?!"

"I booked us a room just in case you want to hang around here and see Chicago."

"Where?"

"I hear Oprah likes the Omni Hotel, so I booked a room there."

Jenna went along with the proposal to stay in Chicago that night with Cwizzy. But she felt a little nervous about the sleeping arrangements. When they got to the hotel, Cwiz assured her that he had booked a two-bedroom suite. He told her the master bedroom was all hers, and that he would sleep in the other room. They spent the next day tooling around Chicago and flew home together the following day.

When they got home, Cwiz called me up and said he had made a decision. He was going to propose, and he wanted me to come along ring shopping with him. The two of us went to Tiffany's at South Coast Plaza to buy the ring.

In the car on the way, I asked him, "Are you sure about this?"

He looked earnest. "She is the one. No question."

I had never seen him like this with anyone, and I could not have been happier for him.

LIFE LESSON:

When you've found your person, never stop surprising them.

CHAPTER 51

THE REVERSE SURPRISE BIRTHDAY PARTY

You would have expected Cwiz's proposal to Jenna to have been the most earth-shattering spectacle the world has ever seen, right? One imagines Cwiz and Jenna standing on the rim of New Zealand's highest volcano, the Mormon Tabernacle Choir singing the Hallelujah Chorus behind them, while Bono skydives from a hot air balloon to deliver Jenna's ring. But, for once, Cwiz did not go that route. Not exactly, anyway. The proposal itself was understated and sweet, but the day was epic.

About two weeks before the day of the proposal, unbeknownst to Jenna, Cwiz told all of her friends and family that he wanted to throw her a surprise party for her birthday. He told everyone the plan was to be at his house at lunchtime, and to surprise her when they returned from brunch at the beach.

Cwiz invited everybody—Jenna's work friends, her family, his friends and family. He even flew out two of Jenna's best friends who were then living out of state (Carolyn from Hawaii and Emily from Texas) for the party. Everyone coming to the party thought they were there for the birthday celebration. But Cwiz's idea was that this was going to be a reverse surprise party. It would be a surprise birthday party for Jenna, but it would also be a surprise engagement party for everyone else.

Jenna's birthday was on a Sunday that year. Jenna drove down to Cwiz's place and the plan was that they would go to church together that morning but get breakfast first. Instead of going to their usual bagel spot next to the church, Cwiz turned toward the freeway and started heading south. Jenna asked what was up, and he said they should do a more special breakfast on her birthday.

On the way south, Cwiz's car blew out a tire. *Seriously? Today?* he thought to himself.

Cwiz got out to inspect the flat, thought about it for a second, and realizing the last thing he wanted to do was get all hot and sweaty changing a tire right before a proposal, he called for help.

Cwiz called Trav, who was just waking up. "Dude, I need you."

Trav said sleepily, "What's going on?"

"I need you to hop in your car right now and drive down the 73 south toward Laguna. I'm broken down on the side of the road right now and I need your car."

Trav said without hesitating, "Okay, be there in fifteen."

Trav hopped out of bed and was there within fifteen minutes as he promised. They switched cars. Trav then waited for the tow truck while Cwiz and Jenna drove off on their big day. Jenna thought it was weird that Trav was just waiting with their car for the tow truck, and that he switched cars with them like that. *My friends wouldn't do that. They would just tell me to wait for the tow truck. That is amazing!* Despite thinking it was a little weird, she was none the wiser about what a special day this was.

As an aside, when I interviewed Trav about the day of the proposal, I asked Trav why he got out of bed and rescued Cwiz with no questions asked like that. Trav replied, "The dude took me to lunch practically every day for ten years and he never let me pay one time. What am I gonna say? No?"

Cwiz and Jenna drove Trav's Camry to the St. Regis Hotel. It was a beautiful, sunny October morning. They walked up and told the hostess they had a reservation. The hostess looked at Cwiz knowingly and said they needed about fifteen minutes to get the table ready. Jenna was a little annoyed. I mean, what is the point of a reservation? But Jenna did not know that Cwiz had asked the hostess to do this, to give him an excuse to take Jenna on a little walk and propose before brunch.

They walked down to a garden at the hotel. The grounds had

been set up for a wedding, and it was gorgeous. Jenna commented on how beautiful it was.

Cwiz gave her a long hug and said, "I love you so much. I am really excited for the amazing life we are going to have together."

Jenna replied, "I love you too."

Then he suddenly got on one knee.

"Will you marry me?"

Jenna was not expecting this, but there was no hesitation when she said "Yes!" and watched him put the ring on her finger. The brunch was that much better with a ring on, and she stared at it in amazement.

Best birthday present ever, she thought.

They drove back in Trav's car to Cwiz's house. Just before they opened the door to the house, Cwiz said to her, "Remember, no one knows we're engaged."

Jenna did not compute what he was trying to tell her, and when he opened the door, a resounding "SURPRISE!" rang out. Everyone rushed up to give her a hug. But before they could get their arms around her, Cwiz said to everyone, "Thank you, everyone, for coming. And now we have a surprise for you. We're engaged!"

Their friends and family freaked out. The double surprise worked perfectly.

Later that night, after everyone had gone, Cwiz sat down with Jenna and they snuggled and talked about the amazing day they had, how each of their friends reacted to the news, and how scrumptious the caterer's carne asada was.

Cwiz then said, "I have one more surprise for you. Wait here."

Jenna wondered what more there could possibly be.

Cwiz went to his closet and pulled out a plastic storage bin.

Cwiz sat back down next to her and said, "This is yours. It has a lot of things in it, so I need to help you unpack it. And I need to explain what it all is. Okay?"

Jenna said, "Of course. What's in it?"

The items in the bin were organized oldest to newest, and Cwiz pulled out the oldest item first. It was a letter he wrote to his future wife in 1997, while he was alone in Turkey. The envelope was addressed "To my future wife." It was now 2006. In the letter, he wrote that he was going to pray for her, whoever and wherever she was, that he was going to prepare for a life with her, and that he could not wait to live his life someday with her.

Cwiz told Jenna that after he wrote that letter, whenever he thought about his future wife, or his future life as a married man, he picked up a memento and threw it in the bin, and he'd been collecting things since then, for the last ten or so years. He decided someday he would present the box to her, whoever she would be.

Cwiz told her, "Now I know this is all yours."

He showed her several Christmas ornaments that he had bought over the years in various countries. He told her that he bought these ornaments thinking of the tree that someday they would put up at Christmas in their home.

There were women's soccer jerseys that he had picked up over the years in several different countries. (Jenna just so happens to be a soccer player.) There were also several other letters he had written to his future wife, at various times in his life, when he was feeling lonely or wondering whether he would ever meet her. The letters imagined what their lives might be someday.

Jenna looked in the bin for what was left. She found a box of Samoas Girl Scout cookies. On the back of the box, Cwiz had scrawled a note years earlier. The note said, "Every time I buy one of these boxes, I dream about the daughter we will have someday."

LIFE LESSON:
Write down your dreams and make them happen.

CHAPTER 52

MAUI'D

Cwiz and Jenna were engaged in October and wanted to get married the following summer, on July 7, 2007. I found the date a tad odd for a guy who liked to play craps as much as he did, with the number 7 being the unluckiest number in the game, but I let it be. The two of them wanted to get married quickly, and Cwiz started researching how much it would cost to have Julio Iglesias come and perform at the wedding. Yes, you read that right. That was what he wanted to do.

Why not, right? In 2007, the real estate market was going berserk, and Cwiz's business was crushing it. Like a lot of real estate practitioners in 2007, he had excess cash, and he wanted to throw an absolutely huge wedding. He went into planning mode, put together a massive guest list, and put down a deposit at a very expensive local venue with a huge stage.

Cwiz saw himself in his mind's eye, halfway through the wedding reception, walking onstage and saying, "Ladies and gentlemen, I have a little surprise for you. All the way from his home in Spain, Juliooooooo Iglesiasssssss!" The crowd would look around stunned and bewildered, and Julio would launch into "To All the Girls I've Loved Before."

Cwiz was giddy just thinking about all the fun possibilities a huge wedding reception could bring, and all the ways he could make his buddies laugh. He looked into a band, the flowers, the guest list, the food, the whole thing.

But when he and Jenna started talking about what they wanted most in a wedding, they realized what they really wanted was to be able to spend quality time with the people they loved. And the thing that kept coming up when they talked to other married friends was that for the bride and groom, a wedding reception was often busy and hectic, taken up with running from one thing to the next while friends and family partied and caught up with one another.

The excitement of having a big wedding and an over-the-top reception started to fade. They knew they needed to figure out a way to spend time with the people they loved the most and to get all they could out of the whole experience.

The solution was to have a big wedding at the church with everyone invited, followed by a low-key cake reception after the service, right there on the church grounds. The money they saved by not hiring Julio Iglesias could be funneled toward a killer honeymoon—a truly epic celebratory trip. They could fly their entire wedding party, plus their families on both sides, to Maui for nearly a week. They could also foot the bill for everyone's hotel at the Sheraton on Ka'anapali Beach. After making this big decision, they also decided July was too long to wait for that kind of fun, so they moved up the wedding date to the spring and told their families and the wedding party to set aside a week in April for a trip to Hawaii.

The wedding date arrived. The church was packed with everyone that the two of them had ever known. The Captain and I were Cwiz's best men, and we each gave an open-air speech on a makeshift stage on the church patio while everyone mowed down cake.

They did not even hire a videographer for the wedding, instead deciding to give a camcorder to a guy named "Sachmo," who was responsible for filming the day. Trav was given a microphone and tasked with interviewing folks during the cake reception. To no one's surprise, Trav spent his time "interviewing" Jenna's college friends, essentially gifting Cwiz and Jenna with a one-hour video tutorial of how to flirt with girls at a wedding.

The following morning, fifty or so celebrants packed onto the same plane. Cwiz riled us up for the five-hour flight and sweet-talked the flight attendants into giving him the microphone. He yukked it up as usual, and the other lucky passengers on the flight participated in the ongoing celebration.

During that week, Cwiz had planned for us to participate in two group events: a sunset cocktail cruise and a snorkeling trip. Other than that, the entire group basically just hung out at the pool and relaxed.

The amazing thing was that this trip was made possible by Cwiz and Jenna's wedding budget. Here they were, giving a massive wedding gift to all of us, instead of the other way around. And given how they have lived their lives ever since, this was a fitting way to begin their marriage.

LIFE LESSON:
It is better to give than to receive.

CHAPTER 53

MAGNETIC PERSONALITY

For about a decade, Cwiz and I found ourselves on different life tracks. I had gotten married, had my daughter Maddie, and gotten divorced, all before Cwiz married Jenna. So while I was married, he was not, and while I was raising a child, Cwiz was still raising hell. This disconnect in our daily duties and responsibilities had a tendency to pull us apart, to some degree. We were focused on different things.

The funny thing is that almost immediately after I was divorced, Cwiz was planning his marriage to Jenna. And not long thereafter, Cwiz and Jenna started talking about having a baby. By the time Cwiz and Jenna had their first child, a son named Eli Danger (yes, "Danger" is his actual, legitimate, it's-on-the birth-certificate middle name), Maddie was not a baby anymore. She was into playdates, not play mats. So, once again, we were not quite on the same track.

When I met Bri and got married again several years later, Cwiz was constantly telling us to have a baby. He wanted our babies to crawl around on the same floor together. Cwiz strongly, even annoyingly, encouraged us to get started, for years. Meanwhile, he and Jenna popped out their second child, a son named Miller Wylde, and then their third came along, a daughter named Piper Moxie. Cwiz marveled at how Piper looked a lot like the little girl on the box of Samoas that he put in the plastic storage bin years before. He was smitten and loved his role as a dad.

And all this time, Cwiz begged Bri and me to have a child so that all the little munchkins could flail around together. As Piper got older, Cwiz told me to hurry up. Eventually, we were ready, and then Bri was suddenly pregnant.

We went to dinner with Cwiz and Jenna and a few other friends to give them the good news that we were adding to the family. We were at a local Mexican joint. A large basket of chips and a few small saucers of salsa sat on the table between us. When we broke the news that we were pregnant, Cwiz lost his mind. He took the basket of chips and threw the entire thing in the air. Chips rained down on the table and shattered all over the restaurant's patio.

Jenna said, "What is wrong with you!" Then she promptly stood up with tears and a smile and hugged Bri, who picked chip fragments out of Jenna's hair.

Cwiz was stoked beyond belief that a baby was coming. He gave me a hug, and I was surprised to see he looked a tad embarrassed at his chip outburst. He sulkily picked the chips up off the ground and apologized to the waiter ("So sorry, I got a little carried away") as we excitedly disclosed all the details.

Several years later, our munchkins were playing together at Cwiz's house. My four-year-old Kate was absolutely transfixed. She was in Cwiz's garage/playroom, with her knees and legs folded under her impossibly tiny bottom, her flowery dress obscuring her entire lower half. She was focused on building a house made of tiles. The tiles were magnetized, which provided nearly infinite possibilities of configurations. Her intense gaze was on the fledgling structure, and her hair hung down in a tangled mess.

Because I had not seen or heard from her in perhaps ten or fifteen minutes, I went in to check on her. When I walked up behind her, I watched her closely for a minute. Seeing her focus like this was unusual, so I decided to leave her alone with her creative juices, preferring not to interrupt her architectural schemes. Eli, Miller, and Piper flailed around Kate, playing various games, but Kate was not to be disturbed.

Inside, I mentioned to Cwiz and Jenna how focused Kate was on the magnet tiles. We had never seen these magnet tiles before, and we asked where they had gotten them. When it was time to go, we had to pry Kate away from the tiles. We promised her she would have another chance to play with them the next time we came over. While we negotiated with her in the garage, Uncle Giggles watched this play out, amused.

The next day, after school, Kate was drawing at our kitchen table. There was a knock on the door. When Bri opened it, an Amazon package lay on the welcome mat. It was addressed to "Katie-McKate Kates."

Inside was a brand new package of magnet tiles. The card inside said, "For Kate, from Uncle Giggles."

LIFE LESSON:
Chips are not confetti.

CHAPTER 54

REMODEL SURPRISE

H aving kids has a way of focusing you on what is important. That is not always the case, of course, but it was with
Cwiz. After his kids were born, it was obvious to me that Cwiz
started to channel his energies and talents in a direction he deemed
most important to meet his goals. He was focused on growing his
businesses, but not for the mere purpose of making money. Cwiz
viewed the money, and even the businesses themselves, as a tool
to reach a higher purpose. He wanted to give his family, and the
other people around him, experiences that they would remember
their whole lives. He was all about making memories.

Case in point: a family hired Cwiz to complete a remodel of
their home. It was September, and because it was a total remodel,
Cwiz told them he would probably need until January to complete
the job, or a full four months. The dad, Steve, considered this to
be entirely reasonable considering the scope of the project. But
Steve privately thought that the job would take much longer. After
all, contractors always take longer than they say, so he figured it
would be a six-month job, minimum. Cwiz told the family to plan
on being out of the house until at least January, and he also asked
them not to peek at the house while the work was in progress.

Unbeknownst to Steve and his family, however, Cwiz had decided he was going to surprise them. Cwiz wanted to do something
special. Cwiz was aware that Angelica, Steve's wife, had suffered
through a bout of breast cancer the year before, and the medical
scare had set the family back for quite some time. Cwiz was hoping
he could knock out the remodel in record time and get them back
to normalcy, and with a beautiful new home. He also planned

to do work they did not expect him to do, to beautify the home beyond their expectations.

Cwiz's crew at Grason Construction went to work like bees. Cwiz monitored the progress daily and they finished the job in just seventy-two days, in November, well ahead of schedule. The finished product included the work they expected, but Grason also added backyard features that were not on the plans, including complete landscaping.

For a personal touch, Cwiz added a built-in barbecue feature and called it Cooper's Grill, after their son Cooper. In addition, my wife Bri went over to add design elements to the kids' rooms and bought some furniture at Cwiz's expense for every room in the house.

Once it was complete, months before the family expected, Cwiz contacted Steve's neighbors and had them call the family up to meet them for frozen yogurt one night. But it was a ruse. When the family showed up for yogurt, Cwiz just happened to be there with Eli, Miller, and Piper.

Cwiz said, "What are you guys doing here?"

Steve said, "No way! Hey, Caesar. We were supposed to meet some neighbors here."

Cwiz said, "Well, since you're here, do you want to go by the house real quick and see the progress? I need you to make a call on a couple things, actually, so it's good you're here. And then you can come right back."

They all drove over to the house, expecting to find the home perhaps fifty percent done, if they were lucky.

But the entire remodel was complete.

Cwiz said, "Welcome to your new home."

Their jaws hit the floor.

LIFE LESSON:
Underpromise and overdeliver.

CHAPTER 55

THE SKINNY ON TIO FLACO'S TACOS

As you know, Cwiz spent some time in Mexico after he graduated from high school, building houses for the poor. Seemingly every day that summer, he wandered through the dirty streets to a street vendor cooking up asada over a wood fire. The vendor folded the asada into a small corn tortilla the size of his palm. He then threw a handful of chopped onions, a smattering of cilantro leaves, and a dollop of smooth guacamole on top.

Cwiz was obsessed with these tacos, and they sustained him the entire summer. And since that time, he tried to find tacos that could rival that street vendor in Mexico, or at least come close. But such tacos did not exist in SoCal.

Eventually, when Cwiz finally had the means, he decided he would open up his own taco shop and cook his own asada over a wood fire. And he would do it in Fountain Valley, where he had lived his entire life, just a few blocks from where he grew up. That is how Tio Flaco's was born, from a lifelong desire to eat wood-fired Tijuana-style tacos in Fountain Valley.

The food is really good at Tio Flaco's, and they have a green octopus as a mascot, so there's that. But what I love most about Tio Flaco's is that it is an extension of Cwiz's personality. It is yet another way for Cwiz to reach people and make an impact on his world. With the restaurant, Cwiz has found one more mechanism to do good for the people around him.

Four years ago, a tragic death occurred in Cwiz's church community. A father died, leaving his wife and three kids brokenhearted and financially without a safety net. Cwiz and Jenna knew the family well, having sent their kids to daycare in the family's home and having gone to church with them for years. The man's wife also worked part time at Tio Flaco's.

Cwiz and Jenna started actively looking for ways to help this family and decided a fundraiser at Tio Flaco's would be the most immediate and impactful way they could help. They got to work organizing the event.

They promoted the event to the church family, on Tio Flaco's social media pages, and on their personal social media. The word got out quickly. Cwiz had to figure out how to get permission to hold the event, because the Tio Flaco's parking lot would not accommodate hundreds of people coming all at one time. So Cwiz talked to his business neighbors to get them on board, and all of them were enthusiastic about helping.

When the day of the fundraiser arrived, Cwiz had all hands on deck, and hundreds of people showed up. The line for tacos went out the door, down the parking lot, and looped a hundred yards down the street. People waited in line for an hour and a half to get their grub. Thankfully, one taco at a time, and over an eight-hour period, they were able to raise $11,000 for the family.

Cwiz was always looking for ways to increase his impact on people through the restaurant. The first year the restaurant was open, Cwiz decided they should have a holiday party. A few days before Christmas, he took all of his employees to a restaurant, where they celebrated. Cwiz shared his superior karaoke skills with them and picked up the bill. When dinner was ending, Cwiz told them they were all going to Target. He gave each of them money for a spending spree to get gifts for their families for Christmas. His employees were in total shock, and some were in tears, thankful that they could give their kids the best Christmas they had ever had.

LIFE LESSON:
Tacos can change lives.

CHAPTER 56

THE CHICKEN MAN COMETH

You know those public storage units where you pay a supposedly small monthly fee to store your priceless elementary school soccer trophies, beloved stuffed animals, baby pictures, and VHS videotapes? Well, if you stop paying your monthly fees, the landlord will evict your preschool teddy bear Twinkles and sell the entire unit and all of your crap at a public auction. They cut off the lock, open up the unit, and auction off the items therein to the highest bidder.

There was a reality show based on this world of auctioning storage units. The show was simple in its premise. They would follow some of the local storage unit buyers around, film the auctions, and focus on the person who made a big score on something within the unit.

Cwiz and Jenna were in bed one night watching the show. Cwiz noted with interest that the auction was taking place in Huntington Beach. There were regulars on the show who were featured each week, the "stars" of the show, if you will. One of the guys, a dude named Dave whose signature was to shout "Yuuuuuuup" when he wanted to bid, had a shop in Costa Mesa, just around the corner from Cwiz's house.

It occurred to Cwiz out of the blue that since these were public auctions, and because they were filming locally, he should go down and get on the show.

He said to Jenna, "I think I'm gonna go down and get on the show."

Jenna looked at him and laughed. "You're gonna get on the show?"

Cwiz mimicked Dave, a regular from the show: "Yuuuuuuuuuuup."

Jenna was not amused. "What, you think you're just going to walk in and the producers are going to be like, 'Hey there, want to be on the show? No problem, we have a spot for you right here.'"

"Well, now that you put it like that. Yeah, that's exactly what I think is going to happen."

Now that Jenna had issued a challenge, it was on! He started researching when the public auctions would be occurring. He saw that there were maybe a dozen auctions every weekend in Orange County.

Cwiz put on his investigative hat and figured that because the show would want to film as much as possible to increase the chances of a really good unit, the show would tape only at the storage centers with a large number of auctions in one day. In other words, if one center had three auctions scheduled on a particular day, and another center had fifteen auctions scheduled for the same day, he figured the show would tape at the storage center with fifteen.

When he had narrowed down the centers with the most auctions, he called them up. He quickly learned that the people answering the phones at the centers were not permitted to say whether the television show was taping that day, so after a little trial and error, he learned how to crack the code.

Cwiz would call the day before the scheduled auctions and say, "Hi there. I'm planning on coming down from Barstow with my truck and trailer tomorrow to attend the auctions. But last time I did, that TV show was taping and it took forever. I don't want to waste my time driving down with my trailer if you're taping tomorrow."

The person at the center would say, "Well, maybe don't bother tomorrow then. Come next time."

"Okay, thanks for the heads up."

Cwiz showed up bright and early the next day for the show. On his first day at the auctions, Cwiz found himself shoulder to shoulder with the regularly featured buyers that he had been watching on the show for the last couple seasons. He had no interest in what was in the units; he just wanted to have some fun and get on the show. And, of course, his main incentive was to prove to Jenna he could do it.

That was the other code he had to crack. How to get on the show? He figured he needed a signature, like the guy Dave who yelled "Yuuuuuup" every time he bid. Cwiz needed his own signature bid noise, and it needed to be funny.

Fast forward several months later. Cwiz and Jenna are back in bed watching *Storage Wars*. Jenna sees her husband on the show, standing next to a guy named Barry, another regular on the show. Cwiz is wearing an Argentina soccer jersey, and holding a yellow rubber chicken in his hand.

The auctioneer croons, "Do I hear $300, $300 going once."

Cwiz holds up his hand with the toy chicken in it, squeezes the chicken, and it squawks "Errrrrrrrrrrrrrrrrr." That was his bid.

Some of the auction-goers laugh. Most look annoyed.

The show cuts to an interview of one of the regular auction-goers: "Errrrr, errrrr, errrr, my ass. This guy's a joke. Call the chicken bus and get this guy out of here."

Jenna looked at her husband. He was swelling with pride.

Cwiz said, "Told you I'd get on."

LIFE LESSON:
If you want to be remembered, you need a signature.

CHAPTER 57

America's Pastime—Heckling

Cwiz does not like baseball, but I love it. One time I dragged him to an Angels game with Trav and me. We were lucky to have scored seats in the first row, directly behind the dugout of the visiting team, which happened to be the Yankees. Arguably the most well-known player in baseball at that time was Alex Rodriguez, known as A-Rod. He and Derek Jeter were a mere 10 feet away from us, donning their away uniforms.

Trav, who is a very skilled heckler and a knowledgeable baseball fan, was letting the Yanks have it. And in particular, Trav reserved the real venom for A-Rod, who had just signed another bajillion-dollar contract with the Yankees.

Trav was yelling at A-Rod, but there was no need. We were literally ten feet away. Nevertheless, Trav screamed, "A-Rod, you're a bum! You could've been an Angel, a hero to everyone in this stadium, but you signed with the dark side. You disgust me, sir!"

I could see Jeter's shoulders shake up and down a little as he giggled at Trav's constant barrage.

Then Trav hoarsely screamed at Jason Giambi while he stood at first base. "Giambi! Giambi! With great moustache comes great responsibility. So disappointing!"

I had been to hundreds and hundreds of baseball games and to the majority of the ballparks in the country, but I had never, not once, been handed a ball directly by a big-leaguer. Cwiz, having been to maybe a couple of games in his entire life, ends up having A-Rod hand him a ball, look him directly in his eyes, and thank him. You're wondering what Cwiz did to deserve that and how he could be so lucky, right?

Well, when Trav was really unloading on A-Rod, again a mere few feet behind him, Cwiz said in almost a whisper, "A-Rod, hey man, don't listen to this guy. He doesn't know what he's talking about. Listen, will you be my Facebook friend?" A-Rod thought this was hilarious, so after he caught a fly ball to end the next inning, he brought the ball over and handed it directly to Cwiz.

LIFE LESSON:
You catch more flies with honey than with vinegar.

CHAPTER 58

SWIMMING WITH SEA PIGS

Cwiz came home one day with six inflatable tube men. You know those things that flap and dance about in the air in front of used car lots on the weekends? Cwiz had six of these bulky items, complete with the electric air pumps, and he was stacking them up in the foyer.

Jenna asked, "What in the world are you doing with those things?"

He said, "I'm going to take them to the Bahamas with us."

"Why?"

"Don't ask questions."

Jenna, accustomed to such oddities, walked away without a word. Cwiz got to work packing the tube men into suitcases for their trip to the Bahamas.

For several years, Cwiz and Jenna had been traveling with several families from their kids' school during "ski week." When Eli, their oldest, first started at the school, and Jenna started teaching there too, they thought that it would be fun to get some families together during ski week because all the kids were out of school at the same time. They started with trips to the mountains where they all stayed in one big cabin. The kids would flail around all week, the older kids watched the younger kids, and the adults would play board games. It was perfect. The annual ski week trip eventually evolved from the local mountains to more exotic locales and Cwiz started taking great joy in planning and paying for the trips.

That is how Cwiz found himself arranging for the families to go to the Bahamas, twenty-eight people in total, all of whom were being flown out and put up in hotel suites on his dime. Cwiz not only managed to cover all of the expenses for the trip, including food and drink, he planned the entire trip down to its last detail. The families going on the trip never had to lift a finger to prepare anything. They simply showed up when and where they were told.

When they got to the Atlantis resort in the Bahamas, every family had their own shared suite. Cwiz made sure that every room was stocked with prizes, T-shirts, and presents for the kids in each family. In order to get all of this junk to the Bahamas, Cwiz checked (and paid the extra fees for) six suitcases, only one of which carried his own clothes.

Cwiz also booked a huge suite where everyone could congregate and relax together at night, as a sort of home base for all the families. On the first night of the trip, everyone gathered in the main living room of the suite and Cwiz passed out the tube men to every family. He called the tube man Uncle Spicy. Every family was instructed to tie Uncle Spicy to the balcony of their room so that they could locate their rooms from the beach throughout the day.

On one of the days there, Cwiz arranged for everyone to go on an all-day excursion. They drove to the airport and hopped on four separate commuter planes, which flew them to the outer islands of the Bahamas. From there, they hopped on several boats and proceeded to various islands throughout the day.

They went to Pig Beach and swam with pigs.

They went to an island full of gigantic tame iguanas.

They had lunch at a yacht club.

They went to an island to swim with sharks.

They played football on a sand bar in the middle of the ocean.

I called up and talked to one of the dads who was on the trip, a guy named Steve (the same Steve whose home had been remodeled by Cwiz). He told me that the trips with Cwiz over the last couple of years had changed his entire outlook on life. He explained to me that, like a lot of parents doing their best to hold down the fort, he was sometimes wary of going on big, extravagant trips with the family. They were just too costly, and he would rather have the money funneled into a college fund, or for a rainy day.

But these trips with Cwizzy and his family showed him the power of a travel experience. As he watched his kids play with iguanas, swim with pigs, and generally have the time of their lives, he began to see how powerful these experiences could be to bond his family and to shape his kids' minds. When they returned home, his kids would never stop talking about it, and they were already dreaming about the next trip.

Steve said, "I've never met a guy like him anywhere. He changed my point of view on life in a big way. He made me want to start saying 'Yes' more to these experiences."

LIFE LESSON:

Even if it's expensive, travel, and whenever possible, bring friends.

Chapter 59

The Honeymooners

In the summer of 2018, a young European couple, the Giardinos, were married. Venezio was from Italy, and Carolina was from Poland. They planned a long honeymoon in the United States and chose to focus on California. They decided to camp in Yosemite shortly after they arrived and selected a campsite on-line. Serendipitously, their campsite selection put them right next to Cwizzy, Jenna, and their kids, who were also camping that weekend in Yosemite with some other families.

When they arrived in Yosemite, the Giardinos went on a hike, astounded by the beauty of the valley. When they got back to the campground, they were both famished, especially Carolina. Unbeknownst to them at the time, Carolina was pregnant with their first child, and she was gonna eat her own foot if she did not get something to eat, and fast. Venezio promised to get a fire going and cook some steaks.

He went to work on the campfire but no matter how hard he tried, the wood would not catch. The twigs and grass flared up and went out. The wood was too wet, and the steaks would never be cooked. To make matters worse, Carolina could smell the enticing aroma of charred meat coming from the next campsite and could see a perfect blazing fire. She was getting annoyed.

From his campsite, Cwiz watched as this young couple struggled to get their fire going. About a dozen people were gathered around his roaring fire. He was cooking asada and tri-tip over a homemade grill with perfect coals, diligently arranged to create an even temperature. Cwiz was in his happy place, hunched over a cutting board like the Argentine he was, slicing meat with a chef's knife, and passing it onto plates. He was licking his lips and making noises as he sliced each piece. This was his element.

Venezio too couldn't help but notice the flames and crackling pops of the wood at the next campsite. Carolina looked over and saw the meat and gave Venezio a look. *Get the fire going already!*

Cwiz saw them steal a glance, dropped his knife, and sauntered over, introducing himself. He said it looked like they were having some trouble with their fire. Venezio showed him the wood and Cwiz said, "Say nothing more."

Cwiz walked back to his campsite and came back with a huge stack of perfectly dry wood. "This will work for ya."

The couple thanked him profusely, and Cwiz went back to his cooking.

Venezio got back to work and had a roaring fire in no time. But now the problem was that the fire was too hot. There was no way to cook the steaks over this fire. They would have to wait for it to simmer down into coals, and then rig a grate to cook the steaks.

Again, Cwiz watched what was going on. He went back over. He told them that since he was done cooking, they could use his portable grill. "The coals are ready. All you have to do is put the meat on. You're good to go."

They again accepted and were happy to be shoving steak in their faces within eight minutes. Venezio brought the grill back to Cwiz's campsite when they were done, and they started chatting about where they were from. Cwiz invited them to come hang out with them around the campfire, and they agreed.

Venezio and Carolina had the first s'mores of their lives and listened as the kids all sang songs around the campfire. Venezio told me later, "It was like we were in an American movie. We couldn't believe it." While trying and failing to gracefully stuff s'mores in their mouths, the honeymooners told the group what they planned to do for the next couple weeks in the US. Vegas was in their plans.

As fate would have it, Cwiz had a trip to Vegas planned already and was going to be there a few days after Venezio and

Carolina's planned dates, so he told them in no uncertain terms that they should change their plans and go to Vegas when he was there. The other families around the campfire also encouraged the honeymooners to change their plans and go to Vegas with Cwizzy.

One of the dads at the campfire privately said to Venezio, "Seriously, if you can go to Vegas with Cwiz, you should. Trust me, you will not regret it."

After they left Yosemite, Venezio called Cwiz and said, "If the offer is still open, we'd love to come to Vegas with you."

Cwiz said, "Absolutely. Just let me know when you get in, and I will take care of the rest. Don't worry about booking a room or anything. I've got it taken care of."

Venezio said, "We are so thankful, but you don't have to do that."

Cwiz said, "No, no. Listen, I have traveled a lot and so many people have taken care of me when I visited their countries. I want to return the favor. I want you to know America welcomes you. I want you have wonderful memories here."

Venezio could not believe it but accepted.

As it happened, my wife Bri and I were also planning to go to Vegas that weekend. When I arrived, I met Cwiz at Caesar's Palace and he told me he had two other people coming in that he needed to set up.

"Who?"

"I met this European couple camping, and I invited them."

"Really? You just met them last weekend?"

"Yeah, in Yosemite. They're flying in, and I got them a room."

"They aren't concerned that you might drug them and harvest their organs?"

"Guess not."

The happy couple showed up on a Friday night, right when I showed up with Bri, and we met them in the lobby as Cwiz got them hooked up with a suite at Caesar's Palace. He handed them the keys, and they could not believe it. He told them to go relax and that their dinner was taken care of.

I saw them the next day in the casino. Cwiz was shepherding them to a blackjack table where he funded a gambling adventure. He laid down several hundred-dollar chips at a hundred-dollar-minimum blackjack table and encouraged them to play with his money. When they won the first hand, he made them press the bet, betting twice as much. Though they were uncomfortable and barely knew what was going on, Cwiz directed the betting decisions while standing behind them. I watched this little saga go on, having seen it many times before with various bachelors at bachelor parties, and just enjoyed watching these people soak in the generosity with their unbelieving eyes. They walked away from the table several thousand dollars richer, which is always a welcome thing, but even a better thing on a honeymoon.

Several hours later, I caught them with Cwiz talking to a casino host. Because of Cwiz's betting history at the casinos, he has earned a special card that entitles him to certain privileges that the usual riff-raff like me do not enjoy. As a result, Cwiz hooked them up with tickets to Penn & Teller's show, and after the show, they got to meet Penn Jillette and take pictures with him.

Walking around the casino later with the couple, Cwiz tried to walk them into an unmarked VIP lounge. But because Cwiz was wearing cargo shorts and flip flops and did not exactly fit the image of the typical VIP, the security guard stopped them from going in. Carolina and Venezio started to back away, embarrassed. But Cwiz flashed his card at the guard, who promptly stepped back and opened the door for them.

Cwiz said, "Don't worry, I can kill the mayor with this thing."

The day after the show, Carolina and Venezio were planning to drive to the Grand Canyon and then come back to Vegas. Even though Cwiz was flying home that day and would not be there when they got back, he arranged for them to have an absolutely huge complimentary suite at a different hotel when they got back from their day trip. They called Cwiz to thank him again.

About a year later, while Cwiz and I were in Vegas again on the way to Caesar's Palace in a limousine sent by the casino to pick up Cwiz, I remembered the honeymooners and asked Cwiz if he had kept in touch with them. He said yes, and he pulled out his phone and played a video for me.

It was a video from Venezio and Carolina, both of them sitting and looking into the camera. They thanked Cwiz profusely for what he did for them on their honeymoon and said it was the most unforgettable trip of their lives, and that they loved meeting his family.

Venezio said, "Please come to Krakow with your beautiful family. We will have the place ready for you anytime you want."

LIFE LESSON:
You can never have too many friends.

CHAPTER 60

SNAKE EYES

We were in Vegas again, this time celebrating the Captain's bachelor party. There were ten dudes in our party and, as we do, we took over a craps table at the Bellagio casino on a busy Saturday night. We were generally whooping it up and making asses of ourselves as usual.

Cwiz, with his spot at the head of the table, was making a racket, but the dealers didn't mind, because he was generously tipping them with bets on their behalf. The dice were rolling, and thankfully, on this occasion, we were all making money.

There was only one guy playing at our table who was not with our bachelor party. Squeezed into an empty slot next to the stick man, he was in his mid-fifties, hunched over the middle of the table, nursing a couple of leftover chips. His name was Mike, and we called him "Big Mike."

We were playing large that night by our standards, and in particular, Cwizzy was playing huge. Cwiz was laying down noticeable bets all over the table, and on every roll of the dice. Thousands of dollars were swinging on every roll.

By contrast, Big Mike was playing 25 bucks on the "Pass Line"—the safest bet on the table—and just waiting for the dice to decide the fate of his $25, one way or the other.

In craps, the dice move around the table, and everyone eventually gets a turn to roll. But the dice only pass to the next person when someone craps out, so, ideally, the dice are moving slowly.

The dice eventually came to Mike, and he became the "shooter." Mike started off strong by rolling a six, and the bets loaded up on the table. Mike appeared nervous, and Cwiz could see it.

Cwiz yelled out, "Give me the hard ways for the shooter" and threw a hundred-dollar chip out to the middle of the table. This meant that Cwiz had bet $100 for Mike on four separate bets, or, to put it another way, Cwiz was betting $25 each for four separate numbers to come up for Mike.

Mike watched the chip land in the middle of the table, and he looked confused.

Mike asked the dealer, "What was that?"

The dealer holding the stick (the stick man) looked at Mike and said, "That guy," pointing to Cwiz, "is betting the hard ways for you."

Mike looked at Cwiz. "Hey thanks, man."

Cwiz smiled. "You just keep rollin' 'em, Mike. Ride the snake, baby! You got this."

Sure enough, Mike rolled a "hard eight" and was immediately awarded $225, courtesy of Cwiz. At the same time, Cwiz won thousands for his own bet, and was yelling out, "Yes, shooter! You are the man!" Over time, Big Mike rolled several more winning hard ways, and everyone was making crazy money.

At one point, Cwiz threw out another hundred-dollar chip for Big Mike, this time shouting, "Snake Eyes for the shooter!" This meant that Cwiz was betting $100 for Mike to roll a 2 on the next roll. It was a 30-to-1 bet, a one-time bet; in other words, a total sucker bet. If Mike rolled a 2, he would pocket $3,000. If he rolled anything else, the $100 bet was gone.

Before Big Mike rolled, Cwiz threw down another $100 chip and said, "And the same for me!" Several others of us threw out lesser bets for "Snake Eyes," following up and trying to piggyback on the "juju" Cwiz was feeling for the number 2.

This was quintessential Cwiz, always playing like he had absolutely nothing to lose. In craps, as in life, Cwiz has always put it all out on the line, hoping to receive back more in return. His attitude is that he is always playing with house money. And I will let you in on a little secret: he is. Because to Cwiz, it is all house money. That is to say, for Cwiz, it was never actually about the money. It was always about the experience. Cwiz knows in his bones that whatever he spends on experience, will come back to him tenfold.

Mike took a deep breath and threw the dice. They careened off the back wall of the table and rolled gently into two beautiful dots. *SNAKE EYES!*

We went berserk. Travis picked up Big Mike, shook him, and spun him around. The Captain threw up both arms in victory. Hoover shouted, "YES!" and hugged Cameron and me. The dealers were all smiles. Cwiz turned to a strange man behind him, who was playing at a different craps table, and picked him up. The stranger was like six foot three and 250 pounds. Cwiz picked him up in the air and shook him violently, screaming in glee. The man was seriously pissed off and confused. As he was being shaken by Cwiz, he saw the rest of our table laughing uproariously and still celebrating.

When Cwiz put him down, the guy said, "What the hell, man!"

Cwiz just said, "Easy, buddy, we just won huge! Here's a chip." Cwiz handed him a black $100 chip.

The man held up the chip to his friends, said "Alright!" and high-fived Cwiz, and then returned to the game at his own table.

The dealer handed Big Mike $3,000 for that roll. Given his various bets on the table, Cwiz cleaned up more than that. The dealers, too, were making money from Cwiz's tips hand over fist at every winning roll from Big Mike.

Big Mike continued to roll, and his winnings mounted. Eventually, his family came over and found him with piles of black $100 chips and green $25 chips in front of him. I heard his wife ask him what was going on.

Big Mike now had tears in his eyes as he pointed to Cwiz and said, "This guy is winning me all this money!"

Cwiz said, "Are you kidding, bro? You are doing it. You are on a roll!"

At the insistence of his wife, Big Mike changed up and got away from the table with something like five grand. Before he left, we all took a picture with him. Cwiz got an especially long hug from Big Mike and his entire family.

LIFE LESSON:
Live like a gambler playing with house money.

CHAPTER **61**

A Memorable Meal

Not too long ago, Cwiz, the Captain, Amir, and I rented a catamaran and set off looking for a little adventure. We sailed out to the Channel Islands, and after a little standup paddling around Anacapa Island, we made our way across a small channel to a neighboring island called Santa Cruz.

While mid-channel, we saw a light-blue, almost white shape materialize just beneath the calm surface of the water about fifty yards away. It looked like a submarine surreptitiously arriving at periscope depth, hoping not to be seen. For a moment, it did not surface, and nothing happened, but then the shape broke through and a crystalline geyser erupted with an ice-cream-cone-shaped blast. Ian (the actual Captain) had already turned the wheel to maneuver the boat toward it.

Cwiz was standing next to me and I said, "That, my friend, is a blue whale."

"How can you tell?"

"I just know. I can't believe how lucky we are."

I wondered at the thing. We could see only a third of its body, and yet it was still indescribably huge. It lollygagged peacefully on the surface, like some magnanimous demigod of the deep. Having filled its room-sized lungs, it flashed its flukes and dove gracefully back down, into the dark.

For the last ten years or so, I have been regularly paddling on a standup paddleboard in the ocean, sometimes over significant distances, often actively looking for whales. By that point, I had seen just about everything one usually sees in our waters. But not a blue. This beautiful creature was a peaceful, wondrous behemoth, the largest animal on Earth.

I marveled at our luck, but I should not have been surprised. Cwiz had never seen a whale in his life, not in the flesh. So why wouldn't his first encounter be with one of the rarest and most awe-inspiring creatures on Earth? Cwiz always had that kind of luck—or call it karma if you want. The universe always seemed to be smiling at him and giving him gifts. Cwiz was not particularly fond of the ocean, but here he was, being handed a gift very few will ever see in person.

When we made it to Santa Cruz, we motored westward along its coastline. The bright and blue sunny skies we'd enjoyed while in the channel were slowly swallowed by a deep, rolling fog. The gray mass coming toward us threatened to envelop us.

We turned into a harbor and found a place of peaceful perfection. The bay was framed by small mountains of a few hundred feet, covered in coastal sagebrush. The water lapped rhythmically onto smooth stones and shells on the beach. Not another soul was present. As the fog threatened to steal our view, the Captain located what he reckoned was the best spot to drop anchor for the night, hoping we would not find ourselves washed up on the beach in the morning.

Cwiz said, "I am going to get dinner ready."

Cwiz likes to feed people. As proof, he recently spent a small fortune buying a massive pizza oven to be installed in his back yard. The hulking oven had to be delivered by a crane over his house. It cracks me up when I think of his neighbors peering out their windows and watching a 100-foot crane set up in front of their house. *What the hell is he doing now?* I see the oven itself as a legacy of generosity, a giant steel monument to Cwiz's love for his friends and family, because I know I am going to be eating delicious pizzas, a lot of bubbling hot, delicious pizzas, from that oven in the future.

On that blissful day in that serene harbor, Cwiz generously gave me one of the best meals of my life. He had somehow invented a small grill, fired it up, and was carefully grilling thin strips of carne asada, courtesy of Tio Flaco's. There was the asada, but then out came a bucket of guacamole, which had somehow also been packed on ice in the crate for the voyage, and then a huge bag of tortilla chips appeared. Plates were passed around and before we knew it, Cwiz was slicing up piping hot, perfectly salty slices of asada, licking his fingers as he did so. We cracked open some beers and looked at the tranquil water.

We ate meat, chips, and guacamole. That was it as far as the food goes. But it was the company, the nearly silent bay, the lapping water, the swirling fog, and the sound of the sizzling grill that made it the perfect meal. We ate with goofy smiles on our faces, retelling and enjoying the stories of over thirty years together. But more importantly, we relished the fact that new stories were still being created and we were still laughing together after all these years.

LIFE LESSON:
Make new memories with old friends.

CHAPTER 62

MAKING MEMORIES

I was driving my family up to the high desert to visit my father's widow when I received a text from Cwiz. I usually received such messages from him when he was in Vegas. The message was usually a non-captioned picture of some sort: a cityscape skyline view from a hotel suite, an open palm holding numerous black casino chips, a smiling Cwizzy standing in front of some scantily clad street performers with his hand over his mouth in feigned surprise.

Cwiz was in Vegas again.

I responded via text that we were driving to visit my stepmom, and shoot, we were only a two-hour drive away from Vegas. I told him I wished I could join him.

The text came back to me: "Get over here. I got a room for you."

With me were Bri, my older daughter Madison, who was fifteen at the time, and my younger daughter Kate, who was three. I thought about it for a second, wondering if we could make it happen.

I responded, "I'm with the family. We have no bags, nothing on us."

"Don't worry about that. Just come out."

Bri and I talked it over for thirty seconds, and I said, "Okay then, we'll be there by dinnertime."

After visiting with the family, we made the spontaneous drive to Vegas. Just before we arrived, Cwiz sent another message that we should pull up to the VIP Valet at Caesar's Palace. When we did, the valet said they were expecting us and took the car. Cwiz showed up immediately and walked us up to our room.

Both of my daughters were beside themselves with glee, and excited by the energy and hustle of the hotel. Cwiz opened the door to a huge suite. Maddie had her own room with a king-sized bed and her own master bathroom.

"Dad, it has a TV in the bathroom mirror!"

We had a separate living area and dining room, and, of course, Bri and I had our own large room too, where Kate would sleep on the floor next to us. Thankfully, Bri's dad lives in Vegas and he offered to come over to the hotel to watch Kate for the night. This would give us the opportunity to go out for dinner and show Maddie the Vegas lights.

But there was more. Jenna and Cwiz had bags of goodies for us. In the bags, there were snacks, drinks, treats, toothbrushes and toothpaste, deodorant, and hair gel. Jenna had also gone out and purchased Bri, Maddie, and Kate some PJ's to wear. And Kate received the coolest gift of all: a tiny little Caesar's Palace robe that fit her tiny little body. It was adorable.

Cwiz asked Maddie, "So, first time in Vegas, huh?"

Maddie said, "Yeah, it's pretty cool."

"So, what you are planning to do?"

"I think Bri and I are gonna do a little shopping, if you're going to hang with Dad."

"Well, then you'll need this."

He then handed her $200 in cash.

"What's this for?"

"You need to spend this shopping. And if you don't spend it all today, you owe me double."

"Omigod. Thank you so much."

Cwiz then asked her what she was up to these days, and Maddie told him how she was saving for a car and practicing for her driving test.

After Bri's dad showed up and we got Kate settled for her night with Papa, Bri, Maddie, and I joined Cwiz and Jenna for dinner. We were loitering at the front of the restaurant, waiting to be seated, when Cwiz grabbed me and said, "Let's go win some money for Maddie's car fund."

We left the group and walked over to an empty blackjack table where a bored dealer stared into space. She smiled when we walked up and Cwiz put down a hundred-dollar bill. He won and pressed the hand, now betting $200. He won again and stacked up $400 to press it further.

I said, "I think you're good, man. Take the money and run."

He said, "No, this is for Maddie's car."

The dealer busted, and $800 in black chips was pushed toward him on the table.

Cwiz looked at me. "Do we go one more?"

I said, "No way. She will be ecstatic with that for a start to her savings."

Cwiz said, "Okay, let's go then."

He tipped the dealer, and we walked over to Maddie.

Handing her eight black casino chips, he said, "Here you go."

Maddie stared at it, not knowing exactly what she was looking at.

I said, "That's $800 toward your car fund."

She teared up and said, "That is so amazing. I don't know what to say. Thank you so much."

Now, you might say this story is about Cwiz's generosity. There is no question that generosity flows out of him, drenching nearly everyone he touches. But in my view, this story (and indeed, this entire book) is about his unmatched ability to conjure up an extraordinary memory for someone.

Cwiz lives out the idea that when you create a positive, unique, and fun experience for someone, you change their life forever. The experience becomes a memory, which is repeated in stories to others. Each time the story is retold, the hearer laughs and smiles, and the teller remembers it fondly all over again.

This was Maddie's first time in Vegas. Cwiz made it special, and she will never forget it. That priceless memory will remain with her forever.

"*Remember that time...*"

That is what makes Cwiz such a legend, and the best of friends.

LIFE LESSON:
Be like Cwiz.

The Boys. From left to right: the Captain, Amir, me, Cwiz, Cameron, and Cory.

Cwiz, Jenna, and their children, Eli (left), Miller (middle), and Piper (right).

EPILOGUE

About a year or so before this book was published, Cwiz and I were at dinner with Jenna and Bri. I had been working on the book for a long time without him knowing anything about it, but I could no longer hold in the secret.

I said, "Listen, dude. I am working on a gift for you."

Cwiz leaned in, intrigued. "Really? What is it?"

"You know how you've been saying you want to have all our stories written down, and get all the craziness recorded so we don't forget?"

"Yeah?" He and Jenna leaned in toward me.

"Well, for the last year or so, I have been writing a book about your life and all your crazy stories. I am telling you now for two reasons. One, I'm too excited to keep it a secret. And two, because I need your help, and *your* help"—I nodded to Jenna – "to make sure I get all the details right."

He said, "Are you serious?"

I nodded. "Yeah, dude. You are going to love it."

Cwiz's eyes welled up with tears, which I have rarely seen happen. He got up from the table and gave me a long bear hug.

"Thank you."

"You're welcome. Love you, buddy."

Several months later, after Cwiz had read an early draft of the book, he took his boys Eli and Miller on a camping trip. This was during the COVID-19 outbreak, and all of the campsites were closed. When he mentioned he was going camping, I asked where. Cwiz told me he was going to find some isolated spot in the desert off the freeway and set up camp to screw around with the boys.

While they were camping, I was sitting on the couch at home with Bri, when I got a FaceTime call from Cwiz. When I answered, Cwiz and his boys were smiling into the camera back at me.

"What's going on?"

Cwiz said, "We have something to show you."

"What?"

Cwiz held up the carcass of a headless rattlesnake. He shook the tail and it rattled like a maraca.

Evidently, while exploring the hills around their makeshift campsite, they stumbled upon a snake, coiled up and rattling, warning them away. Cwizzy, even though he had nearly been killed doing this exact same thing many years before, decided he was going to show his boys how it's done. Thankfully, this time, he succeeded with no complications. Then they took the carcass home and skinned it. The snakeskin now graces a mantel in Cwiz's office.

I said, "Hold up! Do you realize you have just singlehandedly torpedoed the main message of the book?"

I could hear the smile in Cwiz's voice as the snake continued to fill the frame. "I did? How?"

"Dude. Think about it. You get bitten by the snake, you almost die, then you turn your life around, and you don't do this stupid crap anymore. That's the whole point!"

"No, c'mon, man. It's not ruined. You can just say I'm teaching my boys to face their fears and I am defeating old enemies, or something dumb like that."

"Fine, we'll say something dumb." I shook my head in resignation and then said, "Be safe, boys."

I hung up.

I will leave it to you, dear reader, to draw your own conclusions.

ACKNOWLEDGMENTS

I would say thanks to Cwiz, but since I wrote him a book, we're even. Seriously though, Cwiz deserves much thanks for the inspiration, the lifetime of fun, and the way he went out of his way to promote this book. Thanks buddy.

The beautiful thing about writing a book about your friends and their crazy stories is that you have an excuse to call up your buddies and hear them retell old stories. It is not lost on me how special all of these lifetime relationships are, and so I say much love to the following guys: Amir Rizkalla, Cory Jochems, Cameron Munholland, Dan Speak, Bill Staffieri, Daniel "Reggie" Kim, Travis Terich, Jason Hoover, and Steve Gioielli. You dudes are simply the best (cue Tina Turner!).

A special thanks is due to my particular friend, the Captain, Ian Farrell. The Captain was present for so many of the adventures in this book, and without him, of course, there is no Lizard of Justice. I have no doubt I could write a second book called *His Name is Captain* and have no problem populating the book with amazing stories about him.

The Captain was especially helpful in nailing down some of the historical details in this book. He has been blessed (or perhaps cursed) with an absolute motherboard of a memory. Whenever a detail escaped me in a particular story about something we did, I knew the Captain would remember it. Weirdly, the Captain would even remember the odd notes of past events when he was not present. The Captain is the repository of historical knowledge in our group of friends, our Library of Alexandria so to speak, storing all the knowledge for our little corner of the universe. To the Captain, I salute you, Sir.

I also owe a huge debt to Cwiz's wife, Jenna Ruiz. During the pandemic, while all of us were staying at home for weeks (and then months, and then more months) on end, Jenna repeatedly hopped on the phone with me while she juggled home school and remote teaching, and I picked her brain about her husband. I was surprised to learn many things I did not know about him. I am so happy Cwizzy found you Jenna. You were just the right person for him, and at just the right time.

And speaking of just the right person at just the right time, I hereby back up a dumpster truck of thanks for my favorite person in the world, my wife, Bri. She was hugely helpful with the substance of this book including the structure, style, title, editing, proofreading, and general themes. She was invaluable during the early editing process, and as a former high school English teacher, she was so annoyingly correct all the time, which was an immense help. She is my biggest cheerleader, and in fact, the sexy ex-captain of her high school cheerleading team, so she is really good at cheering!

Next, our dear friend Erin Thomas ("Auntie E"), a current English teacher at Beckman High (shout out to all the Patriots!), also read through an early draft of the book and made insightful comments that guided me as I worked on later drafts. I am grateful to her for giving her time to review this book and more importantly, for her selfless devotion to my family.

My daughter Maddie also made an important suggestion at the earliest stages of writing this book, which I took. Thank you, Mads. I feel so lucky to be your dad, I love you, and I am excited about what life holds for you.

Many other friends took the time to chat with me over the phone and told me their Cwiz stories, some of which I had never heard—the best sort of research. Thanks to the following people: Lori Speak, Scott Graveline, Kim Staffieri, Steve Dobbs, Steven

Dabic, Ryan "Papa" Zachary, Venezio and Carolina Giardino, and Barry Tonge.

And now, to the professionals that helped me along the way:

To Joan Rogers, there is no question in my mind that you took my manuscript and improved it in ways I could not have imagined through your remarkable editing skills. Thank you very much for your straight-forward, honest suggestions, which were refreshing, sincere, and made this book better in so many ways.

To Vinnie Kinsella, you guided me through a new and mystifying process, and I learned a ton from you about how the sausage is made so to speak. I loved our brainstorming sessions, and I am so thankful for your partnership in the creation of this book. Your creativity repeatedly impressed me, and I am so grateful.

To Jessie Glenn, I feel lucky to have stumbled upon you during an unguided internet search, and I am so glad you picked up the phone when I called. Thank you for your wise and sage advice in getting this book out into the world.

To the entire team at Circuit Breaker Books of publicists, social media specialists, and website management folks at Circuit Breaker including Deborah Jayne, Kristen Ludwigsen, Lisa Pegram, Hannah Richards, Bryn Kristi, and Izarra Varela, I have to thank you all for your consistent, dedicated work, and for your creative solutions.

Last, Brooks Becker was of great assistance in helping me in my early editing process. Thank you very much for your early encouragement and making me believe I could really do this.

Thank you all. This was a blast!

THE ADVENTURES OF CALICO JONES

(The complete emails)

From: chungmao1900
To: cococwizl
Subject: Hello Friend

Dear Friend,

I am Mr. Chung Mao Bank Manager of Bank of China, Taiwan Branch, China. I have urgent and very confidential business proposition for you. On November 6, 1998, a British Oil consultant/contractor with the Chinese Solid Minerals Corporation, Lawrence Smith made a numbered time (Fixed) Deposit for twelve calendar months, valued at US$30,000,000.00 (Thirty Million Dollars) in my branch. Upon maturity, I sent a routine notification to his forwarding address but got no reply. After a month, we sent a reminder and finally we discovered from his contract employers, the Chinese Solid Minerals Corporation that Mr. Lawrence Smith died from an automobile accident. On further investigation, I found out that he died without making a WILL, and has no next of kin. This sum of US$30,000,000.00 is still sitting in my Bank and the interest is being rolled over with the principal sum at the end of each year. No one will ever come forward to claim it. According to Laws of Republic of China, at the expiration of 5 (five) years, the money will revert to the ownership of the Chinese Government if nobody applies to claim the fund. Consequently, my proposal is that I will like you as a foreigner to stand in as the next of kin to Mr. Lawrence Smith so that the fruits of this old man's labor will not get into the hands of some corrupt government officials. This is simple, I will like you to provide immediately your full names and address so that the attorney will prepare the necessary documents and affidavits that will put you in place as the next of kin.

We shall employ the services of an attorney for drafting and notarization of the WILL and to obtain the necessary documents . and letter of probate/administration in your favor for the transfer. A bank account in any part of the world that you will provide will then facilitate the transfer of this money to you as the beneficiary/next of kin. The money will be paid into your account for us to share in the ratio of 10% for me and 90% for you.

There is no risk at all as all the paperwork for this transaction will be done by the attorney and my position as the Branch Manager guarantees the successful execution of this transaction. If you are interested, please reply immediately via the private email address above. Upon your response, I shall then provide you with more details and relevant documents that will help you understand the transaction. Please send me your confidential telephone and fax numbers for easy communication. Please observe utmost confidentiality, and rest assured that this transaction would be most profitable for both of Awaiting your urgent reply through this email.

Thanks and regards

Mr Chung Mao

From: cococwizl
To: chungmao1900
Subject: RE: Hello Friend

Dear Mr Chung Mao,

Yes I am very interested. How do we proceed?

Calico Jones

From: chungmao1900
To: cococwizl
Subject: FURTHER INFO

Dear Calico,

I received your email and I wish to thank you immensely for your response. I hope this will turn out be a long and lasting bussiness relationship together. This transaction is 100% safe and legal as you'll get to see as we go along, all procedures leading to the transfer of the funds to your local account or through our correspondent bank has to be secured with strict adherence to statutory provision of the law. As soon as the machinery to commence is set in motion, all the proof and copies of the documentation shall be sent to you in the course of the transaction and as at when due.

Due to the very sensitive nature of this pending transaction, please bear with me if I am being a little vague at this early stage as I am as skeptical as you are with communicating with a total stranger, but please be rest assured that the funds will be backed up with it is not given out lightly, because of my dire need for a foreign partner in this transaction, I request your assistance to pose stand as the next of kin to the beneficiary of the estate of the deceased and all that is contained in the Will as shall be drafted and prepared by a notary public attroney. For this, I urge you to propose a reasonble percentage of the total funds as your share and as an expression of my gratitude for your assistance and partnership, thus encouraging you to guaranty that. I need to ascertain your ability to control and safe guard a large sum of money and guarantee that I shall get my share of the funds from you as soon as you receive the money in your account, I need to following from you: Your full name and address; Your confidential telephone and fax numbers: A brief profile of yourself: I might be able to contact you via telephone and once I clarify your willingness and ability to proceed with the transaction,

Kind regards,

Mr. Chung Mao.

From: cococwizl
To: chungmao1900
Subject: FURTHER INFO

Dear Mr. Connie Chung,

Thank you for your quick response to my email. I have just told my wife about this venture and she is more excited than I am right now (she has been jumping up and down for the past 45 minutes, with exception to the 6 minutes she took to feed the children ... Billy, Samantha, and Facundo) I am glad to hear that this is going to be 100% safe. I have had one too many Amway experiences ... (Damn you Uncle Chip!) One thing that concerns me is that I think we should keep to our code names- remember I would like to be called Mr. Knuckles throughout this transaction. I also think it would be wise for you also to have a code name, how does Kit Kat Mcgee sound? Okay, that settles it- I will now refer to you as Kit Kat Mcgee or Mr. Chiggers for short. I have a quick question for you .... is Taipei anywhere near Jenga?

You had made mention in your last email that there was some sort of machinery involved? I have to say up front that I am on a medication at the moment (has to do with my thumbs) that prevents me from operating machinery at this time. Will that be okay? If so, great. Okay, about the percentage you should get... at this point I feel as if you are doing all the work, especially with the heavy machinery (remember to use goggles) so I propose that we do a 60%- 30% -10% split... you get the 60% I get the 30% and we save 10% (just in case someone tries to get in the way and we need to hire outside help). I have a friend- he calls himself the Hairy Jackal ... I think he is French or from Detroit. .. I'm not sure (but, I have a coupon). What do you think about this split? Does it sound good to you? Do you know the Hairy Jackal? You had mentioned that you would like a profile of me- I will have this to you soon. I have asked a student at the local secondary school to come by with his pencils, spoons, and an easel to draw one for you soon. In the mean time, let me describe myself to you ...

First off let me say I am a Sagittarius- I hope this is ok with you (I am currently trying to get that changed to a Capricorn (not an easy process). I had no idea how much paper work and blood it takes). Hopefully in April I will have a hearing. I like the number 92- not sure why. I am also a huge fan of bowling (Video Bowling, of course). I hope that this is a good start. I also think this might be a good time for you to tell me a little about yourself and your interests (remember I will keep this very confidential and I promise not to share it with anyone)

Personal Information:

As you know my full name is Calico Jones (but please remember that I go by Mr. Knuckles). I am in the middle of moving so I will get you my home information soon. I do not have a fax machine but I am going to try to use the fax at my local arcade (they still have a pole position game there). Would you also Like my social security number, date of birth, and mother's maiden name? Let me know. And one last thing, can you check and see how far Jenga is?

Again, thank you for thinking of me, Kit Kat, and I look forward to my long relationship with you and your beautiful people group. Please say hello to Mrs. Chiggers.

Kindly,

Mr. Knuckles

From: chungmao1900
To: cococwizl
Subject: Re: FURTHER INFO

Dear Calico,

Greeting From Taiwan i have received your mail and i wish to thank you very much of your response, right now i will like you to come up with the old address because it does not really matter wat is more important is to get the funds out of my bank, i will need the address immediately so i can make the document that will make you the so beneficary tothis funds,

I am also very happy of the code names you have gaving to me kitkat and you called Knuckles taht is not a bad id, and i am also very sorry of your medication i hope you get ok soonand about the percentage that is not a bad solution but i wont you to remember that is my dealit ok by me, thank you very much i will wait ofyour update.

Regards,

Mao.(kitkat)

From: cococwizl
To: chungmao1900
Subject: FURTHER INFO

Dear Mr. Chiggers,

Thank You for your quick response to my quick response. I feel as if we are both responding in a very quick manner. This, of course, is very important to this transaction. You will be happy to hear that I have just spent most of my savings buying a very expensive automobile and also a Russian wife for my Uncle Chip (he also has bad thumbs). I figured with all the money I am about to receive it was time to start spending.

About my old address: I no longer live there so I am wondering if it is it a good idea for me to give you that address. (I think there is a Japanese family there now and I don't want them receiving all my money). So what do you suggest? Also, I had requested that you give me some more information on yourself... like how tall is Mrs. Chiggers? Are there little chiggers in your house? What do you like to do in your free time? Do you like fantasy baseball? Can you tell me about your toes? I am still waiting to hear about the location of Jenga. Please let me know what else you need. I am really in need of my portion of the $30 million ASAP (I have a Sears charge card with two late payments).

Also, thank you for your concern about the medication. I have not been thinking clearly for the past few weeks. I bump into many things while driving (mostly older people). I'm looking forward to a quick response (and so does the Hairy Jackal). He has also inquired about the toes.

Regards,

Roscoe P. Coltrain (I decided to change my code name ... too many people were getting suspicious. You understand.)

From: chungmao1900
To: cococwizl
Subject: Re: FURTHER INFO

Dear Friend,

Greeting from taiwan, you can now come up with the new address so i can start working on the document that will back you s the next of kin to this funds. I am 6ht tall, a wife and two kids and my address is NO.162,hecuo siming xiamen china. please remember that this transaction is confidential, tahnk you i will wait of your update.

Regards, Mao.

From: cococwizl
To: chungmao1900
Subject: FURTHER INFO

Dear Captain Crunch (I decided a code name change was in order, pending the upcoming holiday and all),

Well, where should I begin? I want to try and finally clarify what address you would like to send the money to. I have moved out of my old home (the one the Monguls live in) and now I am living at the HoJo's on 5th street. Is this where you want to send the money? I will be leaving here in a few days to move into my permanent home. But before we move any further, I need to ask you a few more questions- I am a little afraid about the transaction and I want to make certain I can trust you, so please answer my questions. Let's start off with my first question- Jenga ... where is it and how do I get there? Next, what about the toes? Are they still in play or has the Hairy Jackal gotten involved? Also, I am very impressed with your height of 6ht- I'm only 5th 7lbs. Everybody I meet always tells me I look like Conrad Baines (you remember him from different Strokes ... Mr Drummond). What do you think? Do you agree? Please answer my questions as they are very important to me.

Also, please give my regards to Mrs. Crunch and your two little Crunchies.

Thank you again for all of your help ... and hard work ... and your fun spirit.

Mr. Octavio De LA LA KaKa (holidays)

From: chungmao1900
To: cococwizl
Subject: Re: FURTHER INFO

Dear Partner,

Greeting From Taiwan, i wont you to understand that as soon as i have you the address and start working on the document this transaction is going to take nothing less then seven working day we will have the funds in your account so i do not no how long you are going to live in hojo's but if you are not too sure you can get me the new address of your home.

I wont you to truth me and i will tel you that this transaction is just of you and i aloan they is nobody involved that is why i wont you to keep confidentailly on this transaction, I wont to ask you a littil question and it is very very important can you travel down to europe i was think to send the funds to a security company in europe because you have to sign some of does document, and also goverment inverstagor can come to my bank soon, and i do not no how realestates business goes will in your conutry.

raegrds, Mao.

From: cococwizl
To: chungmao1900
Subject: FURTHER INFO

Dear Mr. Canker Sore,

First off let me say that I'm a little sad today. I had a nice Turkish rug stolen from my home (it really tied the room together) but I also have good news!!! Today my Uncle Chip received his Russian bride. Yettavictina is her name .. .it is hard to say in English so we have been calling her Yetty. She loves the name and our country Gust not Uncle Chip yet). By the way, Uncle Chip wants to thank you for making it all possible. Ok let's get down to business. As for me traveling to Europe- no, this will not be a problem. I can go as soon as you need me to. I do have a small concern. Why have you not answered any of my questions? (Jenga?) And we have not talked about the toes for some time now- is there a problem? Uncle Chip has nine toes and he is ok with it. Also, you have not been calling me by my code name and you have not used your code name either- why? I do like your name, Mao, but in my language this word means something dirty. I don't want to say what but let's just say it has to do with the zipper zone. Please I beg of you- YOUR NEW NAME IS NOW: Cankles The Carpenter and I will be referred to as Buttons Duke of Mints. So please respect my wishes!!! Okay, now that that is out of the way, I want you to know that those names are going to be kept between me and you and no one else!!! So when do you want me to go to Europe?? Do you need me to send you some money to get the millions out of the bank? Let me know!!! Also, I received a call today from the Yetty's "broker" and he wants to get paid for his "services" ... soI need the money you promised soon!!!! Please, please Mr. Marbles!! Never forget that I love you and nothing you do will ever change that!

Thank You, Buttons Duke of Mints

From: chungmao1900
To: cococwizl
Subject: A BROTHER/PARTNER

Dear Knuckles,

Greeting From Taiwan, i will need your details soi can send them to the security company and they will contact you as soon as possible sorry about your bad news but your good news can keep you more happy, please knuckles i need this funds to be in your account as soon as possible and this is when you are come back (TRAVEL).

I do not need you to send me funds, i have transfered the funds to cu rope so you can pick them up yourself in cash, please confirm the details that you will use to travel to europe and why did you chang my code name but it s also better thank you i will be waiting of your update thanks.

Regards, Cankles.

From: cococwizl
To: chungmao1900
Subject: FURTHER INFO

Dear Cankles,

Thank You.

I want you to know how much I love you and your people. I am waiting for my upcoming trip to see you in Europe (I promise to pack light) but I will bring my trousers (the tan khakis you like so much). I have a bit of bad news- my Uncle Donny passed in his sleep this week and we had a beautiful service for him and a nice eulogy. He was a good bowler and a good man.

301

Okay down to business. I have booked a flight from Los Angeles to Paris, France on Wednesday, March 14th. Is this where you and I will make contact? Let me know. I believe my flight arrives around 9am local time. What else is it that you need? I look forward to our Gay Pari getaway. Also, I have asked a few times some personal questions that you have not answered yet (I want you to know that I trust you over 13 7% but I still need to get to that 142% mark). Please can you answer those questions (Jenga)?! Also, I want you to tell me if you approve of Uncle Chips Yetty- Yes or No? Don't forget about the toes. Thank you for all of yom care, comfort, and support. I look forward to the crepes.

Yours truly, Lando Kardisian

From: chungmao1900
To: cococwizl
Subject: Re: A BROTHER/PARTNER

Dear Kardisian,

Greeting From Taiwan, i love you too i promise to anwser your questions and also i do not really understand does questions please come again, i am very very sorry about your bad news (DONNY) very sorry his he very old now? of the approvel of Uncle Chips Yetty Yes.

I will thank you once again but the security company is in amsterdam that is no longer a problem once you come to europe it will not be a problem again i have to send your details to the security company so you can be contacted thank you very much please keep me posted.

Regards,

Cankles.

From: cococwizl
To: chungmao1900
Subject: Re: A BROTHER/ PARTNER

Dear Canker Sore,

Wow! All I can say is .. .! love you more. Thank you so much for all of your support (Donny). Yes, he was an older gentleman (I use the word gentleman loosely). We have had such a great time remembering our fantastic Donny! My Aunt Gerdy told us a story about when Donny ... when he was a young man, he would kick old people and then throw big rocks at cars as they drove down the interstate. Oh, how we laughed at his energetic spirit. All was good except Uncle Chip was a little angry at uncle Donny because apparently the night before he passed, Uncle Chip caught the Yetty playing "a game" with uncle Donny. He said the game was called, "have you seen my ball point pen". I'm not sure what that means but uncle chip was very VERY angry and the next day is when we found Donny. Apparently he choked on a Jello pudding pop. Poor Uncle Donny ... Okay, so Amsterdam!!! I have never been there but isn't that where woman of the night work? I have to say you are a naughty little canker sore! But, all is well .. .I have changed my reservations to fly into Amsterdam instead. Will I meet you there or should I bring the Hairy Jackal? Just let me know about the questions I have: can you please tell me a little about your family and could you also send me a photo (I can do the same). I feel as if I have told you so much about my family and I know almost nothing about yours. Do you have any crazy Uncle Kit Kats? How about any pets? I had a great dog named Dutch Oven. He was a great dog but one day he bit Aunt Gerdy and she got really sick and pussed up around the throat in a bad way so we got Dutch Oven tested and found out that he was a Desert Rat and not a dog (we couldn't tell because of all the fur). We gave him to uncle Chip. What do we need to do from here? I want to start spending some money, tell me oh wise and gentle leader. Please lead me to the fountains of milk and honey. Let me experience your love and let it flow all about my body as if I was being tickled by a thousand dwarfs. K.I.T.

Your flower of hope,

Tutankhamen

From: chungmao1900
To: cococwizl
Subject: Re: A BROTHER/PARTNER

Dear Cankles,

Please drop a number that i can call you with i have to talk to you as soon as possible and also remember that you have not send your address i think you have to send the one you are liveing now thanks.

Regards, Mao.

From: cococwizl
To: chungmao1900
Subject: Re: A BROTHER/ PARTNER

Dear Love of My Life,

I want to give you my phone number and address but I still have had no answers to my questions. Like I said before, I trust you with my life but need you to respond to my questions. I am starting to feel as if you have another cold sore in your life. I really hope this is not true because if it is I will get very sad and have a rage build up in my life that will hurt all other cankles you have been giving your love to. I hope that I am saying this in the most clear manner in which you can understand (Donny). Okay ... so please answer my question and then I will give you my new address and phone number. Also, in your last email you sounded a little short with me. Please say you're sorry. Thanks a bunch!

The fruits of your labor, Jenga Jones (And what did I say about using your real name?! Don't blow this man!)

From: chungmao1900
To: cococwizl
Subject: Re: A BROTHER/PARTNER

Dear Cankles,

please ask again with your questions because i dont really understand was you are talking about thank i will wait of younr reply.

regards,

Mao.

From: cococwizl
To: chungmao1900
Subject: Re: A BROTHER/ PARTNER

Dear Sir Spicy Pants,

Thank you for your quick response. First off, let me say that I am becoming a little worried that you have stopped using your code name. So from now on I have officially changed your code name to ... Sir Spicy Pants. I will only say this once: do not refer to your self as anything other than Sir Spicy Pants. Let me say it again: only refer to yourself as Sir Spicy Pants. Okay now we move on to business! I have had a lot of questions in the past and you have refused to answer them so let me ask them again ...

1. What is your middle name? 2. Tell me a little bit about your family. (Mrs. Spicy and your little spicy nuggets) 3. How many Toes do you have? (the "T" in Toes should always be in Caps) 4. Tell me about Jenga. 5. Do you know if I am pulling your chain? 6. If you were able to pick your own code name, what would it be? (It's not gonna happen, but dare to dream.) 7. Do you agree with Uncle Chip's lifestyle? 8. (the most important one) You said you were going to send me a picture of you and your family and I am still waiting.

I know #8 was not a question, but just act like it was ok!

Okay, that's all for now.

The dandelion that floats in your wind, Baldavio Anderson

From: chungmao1900
To: cococwizl
Subject: Re: A BROTHER/PARTNER

Dear Cankles,

Greeting from taiwan, thank you of you quick reply do you wont me to anwser spicy pants is also ok my me but i will like to answer the old won,

Question 1, my middle name is zheng.

Question 2, i am married to a very pretty wife and we have two kits a boy and a girl named shing and chang and i love them so much.

Question 3, Toes two.

Question 4, i love sports very well and i am a red sox fans i love baseball a lot.

Question 5, i no that you are not pulling my chain.

Question 6, code name will have been aikon.

Question 7, uncle Chips lifestyle its ok.

Question 8, yes i am going to send you my pie but i to scan it out that is the problem that i am having, but still we are going to see very soon as soon as the funds are in your account i will be coming over to your country with my family.

Now you can come up with the details so we can get down to business thank you very much i will wait of your reply.

Regards,

Spicy Pants

From: cococwizl
To: chungmao1900
Subject: Re: A BROTHER/ PARTNER

Dear Mr. Canker Sore,

Wow. I feel as if you have really opened up to me. I like that you have decided to explore your personal space. I want you to know how much I care about you and that I am touched by all of your answers. I do have one more question: why is it that you want your code name to be Aikon? (If I like your reasons I will change it for you.) I am also glad that you know that I am NOT pulling your chain! At this point I am only waiting for you to send me your picture and then we can start making the money. So please send it soon. So at this point, can you tell me the process as to what I need to do now? I want to get this going very fast (of course I want the picture first). Please let me know soon.

Thank you Canker, Mr. Cwiz-in-it

P.S. I have Toes two too!

From: chungmao1900
To: cococwizl
Subject: A BROTHER/PARTNER

Dear friend,

if you wont this to work out now please send me your detail so i can start worrking on the document and let me no when you are going to europe tahnk you.

Regards,

partner.

From: cococwizl
To: chungmao1900
Subject: Re: A BROTHER/ PARTNER

Dear Flap Jack,

Okay, Okay ... I don't want you to get all bunched up in the . zipper zone! What details do you want and I will send them right over.

(Red rover.. . red rover... Send Chung Mao right over.)

Professionally, Mr. Flach U Lent

From: chungmao1900
To: cococwizl
Subject: PARTNER/BROTHER

Dear Flach,

Greeting from taiwan, all i need is the real name wish i have already than you address that is most important so i can make the document as soon as possible, i do not understand the names you are changing all the time please you can use one code name thank you very much i will wiat of your update.

Regards, Partner.

From: cococwizl
To: chungmao1900
Subject: Re: A BROTHER/PARTNER

So what you want first is for me to pick one code name. Okay I will just have you pick my code name and also a code name for you (from now on we will only use the code name YOU pick). Does that sound good?

Code names for me (you pick one):

I. Yellow Belly 2. Soft Cloth 3. Griffter 4. Hobie 5. Garth 6. Nomar Garciapara 7. Wade Boggs 8. Dr. Phil 9. Crazy Kooter 10. Chung Mao

and please pick a code name for you:

1. Alissa Milano 2. Drew Baryamore 3.Tiffany Amber Theisen 4. Mia Hamm 5. Manon Rheume 6. Amielia Bedilia 7 Amelda Marcos 9. Carol Dalton 10. (you make up your own)

Tell me what our code names are going to be then we can proceed accordingly. Remember, I will always love you no matter what you do.

Love always,- The peaches in your cream

From: chungmao1900
To: cococwizl
Subject: I have not heard back from yo u?

Dear Partner,

Right now we should been thinking of how you can travel down to europe so this transaction can end now, Thanks.

Regards,

Mao.

From: cococwizl
To: chungmao1900
Subject: Re: I have not heard back from you?

Dear "Partner",

I just want you to know that you are not acting like a partner right now! I am a little mad at you because I already told you that I am willing and able to travel whenever you need me to. I can leave tomorrow, with all my Toes!!! You just have to tell me where to go. I will say one thing- I am very cautious now because you have not told me very much about you.

1. I asked you to send me a photo ... YOU NEVER DID!!! 2. I asked you to give each ofus a code name .... YOU NEVER DID!!!

1 am starting to think this is some kind of emotional game you are playing with my heart. Do you really want this to happen or not? Are you just trying to use me like my last wife Fernando did? She married me then took the BMW and also the house we had on the most beautiful lake here (Lake Elsinore) and she left me with about $54,000 in shopping bills. So give me what I want "Partner" and start acting like a partner and not some snotty-nosed kid with his thumb up his HELLO OPERATOR. I will wait for your reply and I want you to know I will fly to Europe as soon as you tell me to. This is a lot of money we are about to share, stop acting like a clown!!

Remember I love you and want only what's best for you my little Chung Pie ..

Peace on earth, Soft Cloth

From: chungmao1900
To: cococwizl
Subject: KEEP POSTED

Dear Hobie,

Greeting from taiwan, i will need you to travel down right now but before you travel down to (Asterdam) you have to take along with you the document that will back you up as the so beneficary to this funds that is why i have been asking you to send the address that will be in the document, that is all i need now, the document will be made and sent to you.

I have pick a code name of you and me i will be answering (MIA HAMM) and you will be answering (HOBIA) so please get the address and i will be waiting of your reply as soon as possible, i will try and send my photoas soon as i am able, but we are still going to see very soon THANKS.

Reagrds,

miahamm.

From: cococwizl
To: chungmao1900
Subject: Re: KEEP POSTED

Dear Mia Hamm,

This is Hobia. I want to thank you for the very nice name you have given me! I like it and so does the Hairy Jackal. Speaking of the Hairy Jackal, he will be traveling to Hong Kong tomorrow and wants to know if you can meet him for tea. Let me know. Okay, so I think at this point I am ready to give you my address and numbers but I want you to first send me a few photos of you and your family (you playing ball or just lounging on the back porch). Thank you in advance for sending those soon. When you send them to me I will be ready to travel. I have next week off from work and I can go then. Does this sound good to you? I am very excited to go to Amsterdam and we can meet there and have fun. We can go out shopping for those cool shoes (the wooden ones). Respond soon!!!

The wind that makes your sail fill with excitement, Hobia

From: chungmao1900
To: cococwizl
Subject: Re: A BROTHER/ PARTNER

Dear Hobia,

Greetings, i most tell you that you are make this transaction diffcult, you are ready to go to amsterdam , that is very good but i wont you to remember that you have to take the document along with you if the document is not with you note that you can not travel because you have to take them down with you.

And of the picture i am having problem in scaning it out, it should not stop you from sending the details, if it s stoping you that means we can not go along to get this funds.

Regards,

Mia Hamm.

From: cococwizl
To: chungmao1900
Subject: Re: A BROTHER/ PARTNER

Dear Mia Hamm,

Okay, here is the deal...You want me to fly all the way around the world so that we can both get 30 million dollars, but you wont send me a photo of yourself??? Well that sounds very odd to me. I am willing to get on a plane for you, I am willing to spend 13 hours on that plane (not including transfers in London), and I'm sure somewhere along the line I am going to have to talk to a French guy (and I hate the French). So I am willing to do all that because I love you and trust you 134%- but you wont do me one favor and send me a photo- why??? I'm sure in a country the size of China that you can find one scanner somewhere (Kinkos maybe?) So why would you not send me a photo? Remember when you said you "loved me too" and when you said, "you wanted to come here and stay in my home and make cookies" well has that all changed? Are you ready to give all that up? After all our history together? All the good times and the laughter? And what about the Yetty? What do I do with her? And what about Uncle Chip? I told him you didn't want to hang out with him anymore (he was not happy). His exact words were," I'm going to go Uncle Donny on him". I don't know what that means but he had a very sharp Spork in his hand. So please send me the photo so I can get on the plane!!! I need the money MIA!!!!

Cool your jets man! Puddles McNoonan

From: chungmao1900
To: cococwizl
Subject: UPDATE ASAP

311

Dear Puddles,

Greetings, ok i will send you the picture soon sorry of the mistake on the name, was i am trying to say is that the document is all most ready i just need the address that will be on them thank you very much i will wait of your update.

Regards,

Miahamm.

From: cococwizl
To: chungmao1900
Subject: Re: UPDATE ASAP

Dear Mia Hamm,

Thank you for FINALLY using your code name! Great news about sending a photo of yourself. .. I will wait for it (I will check my email every 5 minutes). Once I receive it, I will send you all the necessary information to complete this transaction (I am so giddy). I will be having dinner on Saturday night with the Hairy Jackal. Would you like me to pass along any greetings to him and his clan? Just let me know. Also, when should I expect the photo? I am really getting excited to fly to Europe (I'm going to bring my pants). Please send it soon. I cant wait to get on a plane!!

Feel the love ... especially around your meniscus, Calico Jones (aka Mr Soft Cloth)

From: chungmao1900
To: cococwizl
Subject: UPDATE ASAP

Dear Hobia,

This is getting most hard for me to understand.

Regards, Miahamm.

(Cwiz got bored and stopped emailing him.)

SHARE YOUR THOUGHTS

Did you enjoy *His Name Is Cwiz*? Then please consider leaving a review on Goodreads, your personal blog, or wherever readers can be found. At Circuit Breaker Books, we value your opinion and appreciate when you share our books with others.

Go to circuitbreakerbooks.com for news and giveaways.

Jeremy Rhyne is an attorney living and working in Orange County, California. When he is not fighting for truth and justice in the courts, he enjoys standup paddling, reading, running, traveling, and listening to Patrick O'Brian novels on a loop. He is married with two daughters. *His Name Is Cwiz* is his debut book.

9 781953 639028